"Most dreams go unnoticed or ignored and quietly die. Others are noticed but not adequately nurtured, meeting the same end. Yet the God of superabundance continues to knock at the door of our intellect, desire and imagination, inviting us to participate in the restoration of all things. So what a remarkable gift to have such a wise woman, steeped in the realities of dream-birthing, provide us with reliable ways of noticing, nurturing and birthing the very life of God into this world! Beth Booram has given us a healthy incubator, and I light up when I think about the unaccountable good that many thousands will receive from the dreams that are made incarnate through this book!"

David Nixon, founder and director of Sustainable Faith, founding pastor of Vineyard Centra

"God is up to something good in our lives, requiring a prayerful work of paying attention. *Starting Something New* is a timely resource for those seeking discernment and guidance for the secret stirring within that just won't go away. Beth Booram offers both inspiration and wisdom through her own story and the stories of those who trusted the Spirit's stirring to follow after their own God-given dreams. Whether you are seeking direction or providing it for others, *Starting Something New* will help set people on a path they were meant to follow after."

Randy Reese, president, VantagePoint3, and coauthor of *Deep Mentoring*

"This new book by Beth Booram is a wonderful gift to all of us who dare to dream but are unsure what to do with those dreams. . . . Immensely practical, it will walk you through the process of nurturing dreams within a climate of spiritual discernment. Hold this book in one hand and your dream in the other and watch as the Spirit leads you forward!"

David G. Benner, author of *The Gift of Being Yourself*

"*Starting Something New* is a refreshing book of wisdom that promises to support anyone who is daring to let a dream take hold of their life. With engaging insight Beth Booram offers the best of spiritual direction to help us discern God's creative work in and through us and find the courage and boldness to live the dreams stirring in our heart."

Phileena Heuertz, author, *Pilgrimage of a Soul,* co-founder, Gravity, a Center for Contemplative Activism

"As a huge proponent of the importance of dreams and an even larger advocate for the ministry of spiritual direction, I quickly became a fan of this terrific book on both topics! Thanks to Beth Booram for writing such an inviting text for all who wish to discern their God-given dreams."

Stephen Macchia, president of Leadership Transformations, and author of *Crafting A Rule of Life*

*Dave &
Cherry —
God is
up to something new
and good — in our world and
in both of
your lives.
Much
love,
Beth*

STARTING
SOMETHING
NEW

SPIRITUAL DIRECTION FOR
YOUR GOD-GIVEN DREAM

∼

Beth A. Booram

IVP Books

An imprint of InterVarsity Press
Downers Grove, Illinois

InterVarsity Press
P.O. Box 1400, Downers Grove, IL 60515-1426
ivpress.com
email@ivpress.com

InterVarsity Press® is the book-publishing division of InterVarsity Christian Fellowship/USA®, a movement of students and faculty active on campus at hundreds of universities, colleges and schools of nursing in the United States of America, and a member movement of the International Fellowship of Evangelical Students. For information about local and regional activities, visit intervarsity.org.

All Scripture quotations, unless otherwise indicated, are taken from the Holy Bible, New Living Translation, copyright ©1996, 2004. Used by permission of Tyndale House Publishers, Inc., Wheaton, Illinois 60189. All rights reserved.

While any stories in this book are true, some names and identifying information may have been changed to protect the privacy of individuals.

The poem on p. 11 is from "Selection for January 5" by Joyce Rupp, Fragments of Your Ancient Name: 365 Glimpses of the Divine for Daily Meditation *(Notre Dame, IN: Sorin Books, 2011).*

The epigraph on p. 32 is the "Gentle God Prayer" by Corine Murray of the Sisters of the Presentation of the Blessed Virgin Mary, Dubuque, IA (2002). Used by permission.

The epigraph on p. 142 is "The Risk of Birth" by Madeleine L'Engle (1974). Copyright ©1978 by Crosswicks, Ltd. Used by permission.

The prayer on p. 171 is by John Philip Newell, Sounds of the Eternal: A Celtic Psalter *(San Antonio, TX: New Beginnings, 2012), p. 58. Used by permission.*

Cover design: Cindy Kiple
Interior design: Beth McGill
Images: © mitza/iStockphoto

ISBN 978-0-8308-3597-3 (print)
ISBN 978-0-8308-9719-3 (digital)

Printed in the United States of America ∞

 As a member of the Green Press Initiative, InterVarsity Press is committed to protecting the environment and to the responsible use of natural resources. To learn more, visit greenpressinitiative.org.

Library of Congress Cataloging-in-Publication Data
A catalog record for this book is available from the Library of Congress.

P	22	21	20	19	18	17	16	15	14	13	12	11	10	9	8	7	6	5	4	3	2	1
Y	34	33	32	31	30	29	28	27	26	25	24	23	22	21	20	19	18	17	16	15		

To David

Living this dream with you

is what makes it a dream for me.

To Dave and Jody Nixon

Your way of living was my inspiration;

your friendship and support a treasured gift.

And to all

who have a dream inside them

and wonder if it is from God and for them to tend.

CONTENTS

PART TWO: SHAPING A GOD-GIVEN DREAM

Oh, Dreamer who quietly enters my life
With your basketful of transforming symbols,
You come sailing the inaudible night skies
Within the silent corridors of my sleep
Bringing the needed truths I barely perceive
In the bold, glaring light of my active days.
Hearken to me with your messengers.
Gift me, please, with dreams of revelation
So the uncertain path I trod to my true self
Becomes every clearer and ready to walk.

Joyce Rupp, *Fragments of Your Ancient Name*

Selection for January 5

INTRODUCTION

Hope postponed grieves the heart;
but when a dream comes true, life is full and sweet.

Proverbs 13:12 (The Voice)

*D*OES EVERYONE HAVE A DREAM? Some secret ambition or desire that they hold close to their vest and privately cherish? Or are only certain people given a dream by God: some vision of great weight and proportion that they're to give their lives to? I have a growing sense that *many* people live with creative, Spirit-inspired ideas stirring inside them, but have little to no clue (and sometimes courage) how to pay attention to and nurture those dreams.

How do I know this? I suppose first and foremost because I am one who, for the last number of years, has been trying to understand a gnawing urge within me to create something for which I had no name. All I could say with words and capture in writing was that I felt as though God was awakening a seed of something he had planted in me, but I didn't know what kind of seed it was. A new church? A new ministry? A new nonprofit of some kind?

The other source of my growing conviction comes through my practice as a spiritual director. My role is to listen deeply for the activity of God within a person as she or he shares about her or his life and then help that person attend and respond to God's activity. So, as a spiritual director, when I listen to my directees, it's not uncommon to hear bubbling up within them a spark of an idea, an innovative unction from the Spirit, for which they often feel some trepidation, as well as great interest and attraction.

The challenge comes when they try to *voice* their desire, often with a mixture of animation and apprehension, and begin to ask questions like, How do I know for sure that this dream is *from* God and *for* me? And what in the world do I do with it?

Not only do I draw from my own recent experience of realizing a dream and my work in spiritual direction, I have also interviewed a number of people in my own geography and around the country who have courageously embraced, often with great sacrifice, a God-prompted idea that seemed to have their names on it. Prior to each chapter, I will share one of these stories of dreams come to life. My hope and prayer is that as you read them, you will develop the courage to believe in your God-given dream and begin cultivating it with great care.

This book is intended to be a companion guide offering spiritual direction for those who are wondering if they have a God-given dream forming inside them but don't know what to do with it. It's for people who are contemplating an embryonic idea—*starting something new*—but aren't sure where to begin. It's written to provide assurance and coaching for those in the birthing process, a process that feels both creative and confusing at times. And finally, it's written to offer practical help and support for those who are actively tending a God-given dream and need to know how to bring it to life and sustain it.

Each chapter describes a unique stage in the gestation of a God-given dream—from birthing it to sustaining it. Then at the end of each chapter you will find a reflection exercise with questions similar to what a spiritual director might ask, questions that will help you process where you are in the gestation of your God-given dream and how to cooperate with God in that stage. I encourage you to use a journal, perhaps a unique journal, different from the one you use for other purposes, and write and process your reflections and responses.

In addition, I hope this book is a unique and helpful resource for other spiritual directors *and* for those who would like to use it when they meet with one. If you don't currently have a spiritual director and are interested and curious about how to find one, a guide for how to look for a director at the end of the introduction may be of help. Following that is a guide to assist spiritual directors in how to utilize this book with directees who are tending a God-given dream. I encourage you to read both guides in order to understand how spiritual direction and this book might work together.

DREAM DEFINED

When I use the term *dream*, I'm using it broadly. The types of dreams I'm speaking of are quite varied, as represented by the individuals whose stories I will tell. Some dreams involved a change of lifestyle; some a new vocation; others began a new business, organization or nonprofit; and some dreams involved a number of these versions. The following are a few examples of some of their dreams. One of them might remind you of the seed that's growing within you.

- a dream to live intentionally in community with others in an impoverished area of the city, developing a life of simplicity and sustainability, living with less consumption and less waste

- a dream to combine a love of fashion design and a conviction about fair trade manufacturing and environmental consciousness in a clothing design line

- a dream to start an agency that represents the legal rights of an underserved population in a community

- a dream to begin a local nonprofit that teaches young men and women a trade that can lead to gainful employment, and mentoring them as you reveal Jesus to them

- a dream to establish an art gallery within a community or church that brings healing to the city, supports cultural entrepreneurship and celebrates the arts

- a dream to use business and leadership expertise to teach a community in a developing country how to create a sustainable agriculture for growing food and making money for their livelihood

- a dream to help local churches deepen their discipleship and empower ordinary Christ-followers to discover their calling through well-designed resources and training

THE CREATIVE WORK OF BIRTHING DREAMS

So, let's begin by considering some defining elements important to this creative work of birthing dreams. The first has to do with the *tone* of this artful work. You've probably heard it said that dreams are fragile. I think there is some truth in that. But maybe more accurately, the container that holds our dreams is fragile. Our heart contains the seeds of God-given desires. And if we aren't careful with our hearts, they close up, shutting us off from our dreams.

That's why gardening terms like *tending* and *cultivating* seem to best describe the way we care for God's dreams within us. Tending has the same root word found in *attention* and *tender*. If you put those two words together, they capture the tone of our work. We must pay *tender attention* to the seed germ of this dream in order to cultivate it. Yes, like a gardener tending a just-sprouting seed, loosening the soil around it, weeding with care so as not to uproot it, protecting it from harsh weather and watering it, we act as a gardener, nurturing the life form of our dreams.

To protect our dreams we must tend our heart, creating space and giving time for the seed to grow. We must keep our heart pure, uncluttered and clear at the center so that we can hear from God. To protect our hearts, we must be careful who we share our dreams with so that those with the tendency to dash dreams don't dash ours. And we must feed the dream by thinking, writing and talking about it with those who can help us cultivate it.

The tone of our care is important. So is the *significance* of our dream. By *significance* I mean its weight and impact, specifically on the one carrying out the dream. While we might dream about any number of things we would like to do someday—like take a trip to Ireland or parachute out of an airplane or meet a personal hero—the type of dream this book is about is one whose consequence to our lives will be considerable.

If you think about it this way, when you embrace this kind of dream it will *substantially* shape the way you live your life. It will cause you to reorder your priorities. It will more than likely require change—maybe a change of vocation, geography or lifestyle. It will necessitate risk and sacrifice. And it will take courage and belief in God and in you to see it through.

So, God-given dreams are ones that have significance. But don't mistake that to mean they have to have dramatic impact on the entire world to be important to pay attention to. They may not affect huge numbers of people or solve the world's most looming problems. What makes a Spirit-inspired dream so important is that it is deposited in *you*! You are the unique receptacle, and you are the only person who can give birth to it—it's *your* baby! God, who knows you intimately through and through, who has fashioned you inside and out and has been with you through thick and thin, has deposited the seed of this dream in you for *you* to harvest.

This is a good place to clarify the word *dream* in relationship to another word you might be thinking about—*calling*. Are they one and the same? Can they be used interchangeably? I would say no. When I think of calling, I understand it to refer to an overarching life passion and purpose. I hear people say things like "I'm called to be a teacher" or "I'm called to lead people into an experience of God through visual arts." Frederick Buechner is often quoted for his description of calling: "Our calling is where our deepest gladness and the world's hunger meet." So, if that's your understanding of calling, then here's the difference between our calling and a God-given dream.

While calling is also God-given, a dream is a specific application or step toward living out one's calling. Our dream should align with our developing understanding of our calling and be an expression of it. Our calling is discerned and honed over a lifetime, while a dream is embraced and accomplished within a shorter period of time, though we may live into it for years to come.

So, back to your dream. Whether you see it or not, you have the unique capacities and life experiences that realizing this dream requires. You have the passion and perspective necessary to launch this dream. That doesn't mean others haven't been or won't be involved in the shaping and accomplishing of this endeavor, but *it is yours to steward.* And if you don't, the dream will lie dormant or might even die within you.

The tone and significance of this work are important elements, and, finally, so is the *focus.* I believe that to effectively realize the creative work of God within us, we must learn to become narrow in our range of focus. It takes great attention and concentration to nurture a creative instinct. I've learned from my own process that it wasn't going to happen unless I remained doggedly fixed on it and refused to be pushed off-center from it.

According to Greg McKeown, author of *Essentialism: The Disciplined Pursuit of Less,* there's a reason why many successful people and organizations don't automatically become *very* successful. He calls the reason "the clarity paradox," which he sums up in four predictable phases:

Phase 1: When we *really* have clarity of purpose, it leads to success.

Phase 2: When we have success, it leads to more options and opportunities.

Phase 3: When we have increased options and opportunities, it leads to diffused efforts.

Phase 4: Diffused efforts undermine the very clarity that led to our success in the first place.

McKeown concludes, "Curiously, and overstating the point in order to make it, *success is a catalyst for failure.*" That may sound terribly discouraging to you, yet these are important words to heed for those of us who are starting something new. His words underscore why it's so important that when we begin to invest ourselves in a God-given dream, we need to keep our focus, not only in the beginning but throughout the birthing, living and sustaining of it.

On this same point, someone else's words come to mind. Do you know the often told story in the Bible about two sisters named Mary and Martha? Jesus was in their home one day, along with a number of his disciples. He was teaching them when Martha, busy in the kitchen, interrupted Jesus with—you can imagine—a clearly annoyed tone in her voice. She asked him to tell her sister, Mary, to get up from her place sitting at his feet listening to him teach and help get lunch on the table. Jesus responded with some pointed words: "My dear Martha, you are worried and upset over all these details! There is only one thing worth being concerned about. Mary has discovered it, and it will not be taken away from her" (Luke 10:41-42).

I've heard a lot of interpretations of this story, as you might have, and most of the time Martha takes a beating. The typical application is that we all need to choose the "one thing" that Mary discovered—to sit at the feet of Jesus. Well, that's good and true, and there's a time that that is exactly what we need to do. However, we can't remain at Jesus' feet all the time. We have to get up at some point and "get lunch on the table."

I wonder if there's another application to this story. Jesus is really suggesting that "there is only one thing worth being concerned about" *at a time*, and if you discover that, it won't be taken away from you. Mary was embodying the posture of a person who was aware of what was most important in that moment, and she focused on it. She was present. *She was a single-tasker*. Martha, on the other hand, was a *multitasker*; she was worried about and distracted by many things.

If we are eager to harvest the seed of our God-given dream, we must become single-taskers. We must stay with it until it sprouts, watch over it as it grows and feed it along the way. If we try to attend to more than one dream at a time, it's likely that none of our dreams will see the light of day. I learned that the honest way! It became clear that it was going to require more patience, determination and focus than I ever imagined to birth my God-given dream. Let me end by telling you about it.

WAY LEADS TO WAY

It might help if I start a few years back. In 2004 my husband, David, and I found ourselves in a place we hadn't anticipated: jobless. Because of some soul-crushing experiences related to our pastoral roles within a local church, we both resigned. It wasn't premeditated. It was simply a choice of survival. Jesus' words "And what do you benefit if you gain the whole world but are yourself lost or destroyed?" (Luke 9:25) described the way we were experiencing our situation. We came to realize that our souls were at stake. And so we both, simultaneously, jumped ship and hoped that God would be there to throw us a line.

For several years after, I pined for a vocational role that fit me the way my role in that church had fit me. It aligned so well with my passion and gifts. I worked with some amazing and creative people. I saw God do the deep work of healing many hearts. I enjoyed tremendous fruit. So, I did what many do when they have lost something important and meaningful. I kept looking for its replacement. And I kept looking where I had found it before—on the staff of a local church. I tried that twice, hoping that I might find my niche, my sweet spot, but both times I had the sense that I couldn't really root in that soil. It wasn't my place.

During that time, my good friend Ann quoted Robert Frost to me. She said, "Remember that 'way leads to way.'" That seemed like wisdom and resonated with me, that each way, though it wasn't where I would ultimately land, led to the next way and then the next. So, I continued to turn down roads that looked promising and walked through open doors that seemed to have potential. One of the doors was a training course to become a spiritual director.

I met Dave Nixon, the founding pastor of Vineyard Central and a ministry called Sustainable Faith in Cincinnati, when he spoke at our church. In a conversation with him afterward, I learned that he led a School of Spiritual Direction cohort each year, and there was one beginning in just a couple of months. I'd become curious about receiving training to offer spiritual direction after having met with my own director on and off for many years. I'd also become more drawn to ministry with individuals in contrast to the large gatherings that I'd invested so much time and energy toward in my previous roles. So, with a small amount of investigation and a dose of prayer, I jumped on the chance to participate in the School of Spiritual Direction, quite unaware at the time of the significance of the decision.

We met for our first cohort in September at Sustainable Faith, an urban retreat center housed in a former convent. The ambiance of the space was so alluring to me. Built in the late 1800s, it had enormously high ceilings, hardwood floors, exposed brick and generous-size rooms. It was drenched in a quiet spirit that felt sacred—a spirit of peace and welcome. I wondered if all those decades of nuns praying, not to mention Dave, Jody and their community praying, had permeated the atmosphere to the point that shalom was palpable.

As I drove away that first time, I found myself thinking about the experience and even saying to myself, *I'd love to do that*. Well, over time and after many returns to the convent, I began to write in my journal about a desire that was stirring within me to start a similar ministry in Indianapolis, where I live. One weekend, more than a year later, I shared my desires with our house church/small group community. We had gone away for the weekend together, and I hadn't really shared with anyone what I was thinking. It felt big and vulnerable to openly declare it. Would they wonder secretly, *Who do you think you are?* Or would they not believe me that I was serious about it, or think that the idea was dumb?

To be honest, I don't even remember their reactions. But knowing them as I do, I would guess that they were lovingly attentive and took me seriously. Most important, David and I began to talk more earnestly about this dream, imagining what it might be like and being realistic about the obstacles in the way. One thing you need to know about my husband is that he is, without a doubt, my strongest supporter. And he never once questioned my dream—for *me*. He made it clear that he was behind me and would support me all the way, but it wasn't *his* thing.

So, I researched how to write a business plan and wrote one, began meeting with people smarter than me about doing this kind of thing, and began to pray—earnestly and maybe even a little obsessively. I kept writing about my desires and talking with David about what it could be like. The most overwhelming and formidable mountain to climb involved two issues: funding it and figuring out how to do it with my husband's support but not his personal investment.

Then something unexpected happened. I was invited by Cindy Bunch, my editor at InterVarsity Press, to a writing retreat at a beautiful retreat center, the Bellfry, in the mountains of Virginia. David and I had planned a vacation right after, so he came along with me to the retreat. Together we watched Anne Grizzle, the owner and host of the retreat center, as she offered us her gracious gift of hospitality, leadership and presence. The experience made quite an impression.

We left there and continued our vacation, but our conversation kept returning to our experience at the Bellfry. I knew something had shifted within David when I found him on his computer, an hour after we got home from vacation, looking for properties!

There have been many twists, turns, about-faces and alternate routes taken since that time. I will tell you more about them throughout this book. But what you'd probably like to know, and what I'd love to share, is that on June 1, 2012, we moved into a hundred-year-old home in the heart of our beloved city and have established an urban retreat center called Sustainable Faith Indy. Yes, we are living our dream!

A GUIDE FOR FINDING A SPIRITUAL DIRECTOR

If you don't currently have a spiritual director but are curious about how to find one, let me offer a few suggestions that could benefit your search. There are three primary sources to consider when trying to locate one. The first may be obvious, but it's your own network. Think of people you know who are meeting with a spiritual director or would be familiar with directors in your area. Priests, pastors, nuns, Christian educators, retreat leaders, authors and counselors are often good resources.

Second, consider contacting any nearby theological schools, convents, monasteries or retreat centers for names of spiritual directors in your area. It's common for these types of communities to make referrals of spiritual directors to the broader Christian community. Some will even have a training program they offer for those interested in learning the art of spiritual direction.

Finally, there are a few organizations that you can consult online. The first and largest is called Spiritual Directors International (sdiworld.org). Several aids on their website will help you in your search for a spiritual director in your area. Keep in mind that the spiritual directors listed in their "Seek and Find Guide" are from all faith traditions. Another organization you can consult is the Evangelical Spiritual Directors Association (ecswisdom.org/esda/tips). On both SDI's and ESDA's websites you can read about how to find a spiritual director, what to ask them, and how to determine who is a good fit.

Which brings us to another consideration when looking for a spiritual director: what makes for a good fit? The answer to that question is very personal. You will need to trust your own instincts and be patient and determined about finding someone who works well for you. Here are a few questions to ask yourself:

- Do I prefer a female or male spiritual director? Or is either fine?

- From what faith, denomination or spiritual tradition do I prefer my director to be?

- How far am I willing to travel to meet with a spiritual director?

- Would I be comfortable meeting for spiritual direction "virtually"— via phone, Skype, etc.?

- How much can I afford to pay to meet with one?

Once you identify a few names, I encourage you to set up an interview with two or three.

Here are some questions you might ask them:

- How would you describe the ministry of spiritual direction?
- How do you approach offering spiritual direction?
- How many years have you been offering spiritual direction?
- Where were you trained?
- How often do you typically meet with directees?
- How much is your fee? (Some directors charge a flat fee, some ask for what you can afford, and some don't charge a fee.)

Finally, here are some things to think about as you reflect on your time with each spiritual director you interviewed:

- How did I feel in their meeting space? Did the setting feel comfortable to me?
- What was the chemistry like between us?
- What did I enjoy about my interaction with this spiritual director?
- Was there anything I didn't like about my experience?
- Of those I've met with, who am I most drawn to?

I hope that as you explore finding a spiritual director, you will discover someone who is a great fit for you! I think of meeting with my spiritual director as a spiritual practice; once a month, I check in with her so that she can help me be attentive to my own soul and how God is engaging me in my own spiritual formation. If I can be of any assistance in your search, please don't hesitate to email me (bethbooram@sbcglobal.net). I'd be delighted to help!

A GUIDE FOR SPIRITUAL DIRECTORS: USING THIS BOOK IN SPIRITUAL DIRECTION

In our work as spiritual directors we have the sacred vocation of listening for the distant echoes of a drumbeat within a directee, reverberations that belong to the beat of their own heart and God's heart and relate to a unique work they are being called by God to do in the world. We understand that we aren't *really* the one directing; we, instead, are helping others discover the spiritual direction already within them. So, first of all, I want to affirm you and encourage you as to the privilege of your call and the significance of what it can mean for those you shepherd.

In the Gospels, Jesus asked for his disciples to pray for those of us called to this ministry of spiritual direction. Looking out over a large crowd of people, he felt compassion for them because he saw how lost they were. They were aimless and helpless because they had lost touch with the beat of their own hearts and God's heart. Jesus said to his disciples, "The harvest is great, but the workers are few. So pray to the Lord who is in charge of the harvest; ask him to send more workers into his fields" (Matthew 9:37-38). You are one of those prayed-for workers.

As you companion your directees, there may be times when they begin to articulate a hunch about a dream taking form within them. You will notice, as I have, that this hunch both excites and terrifies them. They want to understand it. They want to know if it's legitimate. They want to know what to do with it. And they will probably ask you what to do. (And because you are well-trained, you won't answer but explain that only they can know, through God's help, what it is and what to do with it.)

This book can be helpful for you as a spiritual director as you companion them along the journey of giving birth to their dreams. There are a few ways you can use it. The first is simply to go through the book in chronological order, chapter by chapter, focusing in particular on the reflection exercise at the end of each chapter. There you will find questions useful to the spiritual direction process. You can assign them or ask them within your session together.

Another way you might help directees attend to their dreams is by assigning certain chapters or reading a portion of a chapter to them and allowing your directees to sit with the content and respond to what they are hearing. Again, the reflection questions can be helpful for your sessions.

Finally, you can use this book simply as your own resource for better understanding this creative work of birthing a dream. If you are accompanying someone who is agonizing over a dream and you would like to know how to be helpful, you may want to read this book through or pull out chapters that seem most pertinent to the stage of the process your directee is in.

I am delighted for whatever way this book can serve you and those you direct. May you, through the wisdom of the Holy Spirit, have ears to hear the distant drumbeat and, with reverence, help those you direct give ear to it, as well.

Part One

DISCERNING A
GOD-GIVEN DREAM

INTERVIEW

Abby Kuzma and the Neighborhood
Christian Legal Clinic

*A*BBY KUZMA IS HIGHLY ENERGETIC, hugely optimistic and willing to take risks. And while those qualities would appear to make her a likely candidate to conceive a God-given dream, Abby would quickly say that at the time her dream was planted she was an unlikely person. After retiring in 1989 from her job as subcommittee chief counsel on Capitol Hill in Washington, DC, she and her husband, Ben, moved to Indianapolis so that Ben could start his practice as a radiologist. Abby spent the next several years at home raising their children.

She explained,

I was a stay-at-home mom. I was retired. I had literally given up the law. For six years I spent time studying God's Word, studying with other Christian women who challenged me. It was major spiritual preparation for what was ahead. Had I not been spiritually ready I might not have heard from God.

So, on one fateful Palm Sunday in 1992, at Tabernacle Presbyterian Church, an inner-city congregation with a strong tradition of mission, Abby heard her pastor cast a vision for their church to start a neighborhood pro bono legal clinic. Abby sat spellbound, knowing in a moment's time that God was tapping her to be involved in this work. At the end of the message, Pastor Kik challenged people who had gifts to contribute to seek him out. She wasted no time, and that week met with him and ultimately he asked her to lead the initiative.

This wasn't anything Abby had ever done before or for that matter had ever dreamed of doing. But she knew it was right. As she began to lean into it, one step at a time, she learned by trial and error. If something didn't work, she learned to be flexible and find another way. Her first step was to research how other pro bono legal clinics around the country operated, and then she visited some of them with other interested volunteers.

After thorough research and planning, in 1994 Abby and her team opened the doors to the Neighborhood Christian Legal Clinic. For six years, everyone worked as volunteers. They were open on Saturdays for in-take and then volunteers would follow up on the cases. They went from six to ten to thirty volunteers in just a few years. Then, in 2001, they received their first grant. At that point the clinic had more people coming on Saturday than they could serve, so they opened two days a week. Finally, the clinic had enough income to hire Abby and a few support staff.

Abby shared,

It was a rewarding and difficult—painful process. We were always understaffed and underfunded. I knew it would die if I left. Many times, I felt like quitting, but knew it wasn't the right time. Once we got to the place that we had staff, I had to fundraise to support them. That was a lot of pressure.

Giving birth to this dream wasn't a walk in the park, but there were many great moments along the way. For Abby, asylum cases became her favorites. Nothing was as satisfying to her as serving people who had been persecuted in their own country. She shared one example of a woman who was an activist in an African country, working in a women's pro-democracy movement, under the watch of a tyrannical dictator. One night she was dragged from her car while at the gate to her home, mercilessly beaten and left for dead. Someone miraculously found her and took her to a private clinic, where she was treated. Ultimately, this woman was able to escape the country and find asylum in Indiana through Abby's work at the legal clinic.

Abby and other volunteers founded the Neighborhood Christian Legal Clinic in 1994 as a faith-based, nonprofit 501(c)(3) corporation offering pro bono legal representation and preventive legal education to low income families, including immigrants, minorities and inner-city population. Their main services revolve around immigration, housing, tax and family law. Abby was the executive director of the legal clinic from its founding until 2009. She now works for the Indiana Attorney General's office and focuses much of her attention on the fight against human trafficking.

1

CONCEIVING

Gentle God,
Take my hand and lead me
to the dream that you have for me.
Open my eyes and ready my heart
to receive the gentle stirrings of the Spirit.
In every step of my journey be near.
Amen.

Corine Murray

*I*T SEEMS STRANGE THAT ONE of the most significant and dramatic moments in our lives happens without our knowing it. Quietly, in the deep darkness of the womb, a sperm and egg commingle in secret. Instantly, without fanfare, a brilliant, stunning human life is conceived. And those whose progeny this is have no notion of him or her at that moment of conception.

I suspect that this is also true of those who have been given a dream from God. We might look back and have a hunch when this dream began to form within us. We might identify certain things that were going on at the time that seemed to provide the perfect conditions for its implantation. But when the idea was fertilized, when the tiny speck of a life form came to be, we don't exactly know.

My dream was conceived over a several-year period of growing desire for a better vocational fit. I felt an unremitting desire inside me for work that was more fulfilling within a culture that felt compatible to my values. Something was missing. I would write about it in my journal, trying to name it but typically stumbling over words to clarify or define it. It was uncomfortable to feel. It reminded me of what I had had and what I didn't have at present.

The desire often felt like discontent. Though nothing in life was unbearable and I had work that was paying the bills, I couldn't dismiss or ignore the longing to start something new, something that fit who I was and what I was created to do. I found acknowledging the desire painful at times, like a couple who are experiencing infertility and would rather not speak of the agony of their unmet longings. It's a desperate place to be when you want something so badly but have little to no ability to make it happen.

Coupled with the desire for new life is often the feeling of desperation. The ache of what we want is so strong and insistent we can begin to feel desperate for its fulfillment. While no one would deny the unpleasantness of these emotions as they play tug-of-war in our hearts, they do form within us some very potent and heartfelt prayers, prayers that I believe are seminal in creating the conditions for conceiving a dream.

PRAYER FROM THE ACHE OF UNMET LONGING

Perhaps it was this combination of desire and desperation that provoked Zechariah's prayers for him and his wife, Elizabeth. I imagine him wistfully looking at her, seeing the sadness in her eyes, a mirror of her heartache over never having a child of their own, and praying his heart out. Praying with a fervency he'd rarely experienced, asking God for the improbable after so many childless years, asking God for a baby.

When the angel Gabriel greeted Zechariah in the sanctuary of the Lord as he was fulfilling his priestly duty, Gabriel said to him, "Don't be afraid, Zechariah! God has heard your prayer" (Luke 1:13). What prayer? Did Zechariah even remember what he'd prayed? Was it so long ago that he'd forgotten? Had he stopped praying now that it appeared he and Elizabeth were too old to bother with dreaming about a child of their own?

When Gabriel continued and told Zechariah that God had heard his prayer for a child, for that which he desperately desired, and that Elizabeth would give him a son, it must have been more than he dared to believe. All he could cautiously respond with was, "How can I be sure?"

Desire and desperation are the kindling that ignite the fire of passionate prayer and provide the ripe conditions to conceive a dream. They tilt our heart in God's direction and open its door to the Spirit's flame. It's a formidable task to hold desire in our hearts and the subsequent desperation that comes when we get in touch with the desire. But it is this compost that makes us most fertile and open to God depositing a dream within us.

PALM SUNDAY EPIPHANY

For Abby Kuzma, the preparation was underway several years in advance before God actually deposited a dream inside her to help found the Neighborhood Christian Legal Clinic. She felt compelled to quit her job and create more space in her life for her family. At the time, she had no idea that that space would provide the ripe conditions for her to hear and respond to a very distinct and unique invitation from God.

Abby shared,

> I'd been working on Capitol Hill from 1984–1989 for Senator Lugar and was a subcommittee chief counsel for the Senate Judiciary Committee. I loved my job! But I felt strongly that I needed to quit because I knew I couldn't work part-time—I'm too ambitious. I needed to devote myself to my family. Ben (her husband, who is a physician) was beginning a very demanding job. So, I quit. It was a really scary time.
>
> We'd always wanted to have more children, so I soon became

pregnant. When baby Alex was six months old, we moved back to Indianapolis. Nobody knew me. I was just a wife and a mom—not a professional. I had retired. I went inactive in the bar. I was at home with my kids for six years.

During that time, Abby and her family became active members at an inner-city church called Tabernacle Presbyterian. Abby continues:

> In 1992, Pastor Frank Kik gave a Palm Sunday message. He cast a vision for Tab to start a medical and legal clinic for the neighborhood. It was like a lightning bolt hit me. *I can do this. This is what the Lord wants me to do. I can help here.* I was thinking about it all the time and was one of a number of people who responded.

Though Abby met with her pastor and began to give attention and research to the idea, she also did some of her own soul searching. This invitation both stirred and disconcerted her, and through the inner turmoil she began to pray in earnest.

> The lightning-bolt moment felt like God was speaking to me. I knew. I just knew. I was very excited about it. But then, I suddenly had this epiphany—*Did we have this idea and ask God to join us, or was it God's idea and he has invited us to join him?* After about a year, I had to release it and really submit myself to prayer. *Is this from God and for us?* As I prayed, I eventually felt God's peace and guidance. From that time on, I never felt like the clinic was "my baby."

PAYING ATTENTION TO WHAT YOU ARE PRAYING

As I've scanned my journals over the last several years, I've come across those prayers of desire and prayers of desperation, cries of my heart that began to resound with such intensity that I had to pay attention.

In one such entry, I wrote,

> Father,
> I feel, have been feeling for a few years, something bubbling up inside. I know it will require courage, faith and risk to give birth to this. Part

of the labor pains may be coming from my present ill-fitting context. Lord, help me allow the conforming, birthing contractions of life and my soul to do what they need to do in me. Give me wisdom and courage to believe in your vision within me.

If you are trying to discern whether you have a dream from God that needs tending, pay attention to what you are praying. Not the rote or dispassionate prayers, but the ones that have a quality of unbiddenness. Prayers that overtake you. Prayers that you can't "not" pray. They form in you, not so much from your choosing to think about them but from the swirl of desire and desperation merging together, giving voice to your deep yearning. Those prayers can indicate where God is preparing to or has implanted the seed of a dream.

First off, notice the content of those prayers. What is it you are praying for? What is the nature of your desires? Do they have to do with desired relational, vocational or lifestyle changes? Are they in response to something you've seen, an injustice or need that you can't let go of? What common themes keep emerging as you read your journal entries or hear yourself crying out to God, yet again? (If you don't journal, then how about your conversations with friends?) Somewhere in the content of your prayers are important clues about who you are and what God is asking of you.

Not only is it important to pay attention to the content of your prayers but to the ones that survive time—your persistent prayers. I've noticed that the prayers I don't give up on are often the ones that the Spirit is urging me to pray. Prayers related to God-inspired dreams seem to be irrepressible. Over time they intensify rather than become lost in a pile of things I've talked to God about but have eventually forgotten. These kinds of things take time to become clear. By "time," I don't mean weeks or months. Most people who have given birth to a dream say that they began to pray and think about it years before they saw anything tangible come together to realize it.

So, here are some questions to consider as you reflect on your prayers and discern whether you have conceived a God-given dream. It might be helpful to write down your responses in a journal as you contemplate these questions.

REFLECTION: PAYING ATTENTION TO WHAT YOU ARE PRAYING

- What are you praying for earnestly these days? What prayers can you not help praying?

- Describe the content of those prayers. What do you most desire?

- What are your prayers in response to? Something you've seen? An injustice or need?

- How long have you been praying for this? Has the desire lessened or become stronger?

- What is it like for you to have such strong desire?

- What is it like for you to feel desperate for what you want?

- How do you envision God's attitude or response to what you desperately desire?

- What is the most formidable obstacle in the way of God fulfilling the desires of your heart?

- How have you or might you process this obstacle with God in prayer?

INTERVIEW

Randy Reese and VantagePoint3

*R*ANDY REESE GREW UP in Yorkton, Saskatchewan—a place that might sound remote to us but was clearly within range of God's view during Randy's young life. During his senior year in high school Randy began to consider the reality of God. It happened during his apprenticeship to become an electrician—Randy met a guy named Don, a fellow electrician and a Christian, who took Randy under his wing. Randy noticed something unique in Don's life and his special relationship with his wife, Leila. That's what aroused Randy's interest in Jesus. Then, not long after, Don was tragically killed in a car accident. The shock and loss was overwhelming to Randy, yet the grief pressed him toward the heart of God even more, and he began to seek God in earnest, eventually opening his heart to Christ.

Several years passed, and Randy sensed God calling him into vocational ministry. He eventually attended seminary. Because of the way he had been affected spiritually through several key mentors, Randy naturally developed a heart for mentoring others in their faith. That passion and vision only grew with time and became even clearer years later while serving as the vice president of advancement at Sioux Falls Seminary.

In his role at the seminary, Randy had lots of conversations with pastors. He would ask them, "Do you have anybody who is interested in pursuing a call to pastoral ministry?" Their answer was consistently no. He would then ask, "What are you doing to develop leaders?" And they would basically have nothing to say. "What are you doing to deepen disciples?" The disturbing answer was an awkward silence. Pastors would then lament that they wanted to but didn't know how.

Randy had studied Christian leadership formation while working on his Doctor of Missiology degree at Fuller Seminary. He had read the works of the brightest and best thinkers on the topic. Through his studies Randy had begun to develop a compelling vision for forming and maturing Christian leaders. As he shared his ideas with the other staff at Sioux Falls Seminary, they caught the vision and agreed to provide space on the campus for him to house this developing ministry. They suggested that Randy do some pastor focus groups around the country, so he traveled to eight different locations and presented his vision. The consistent response was, "If you do this, we're in."

But when Randy returned home, the administration of the seminary pulled the plug on it. "So, I resigned." Randy explained.

I knew I needed to move ahead with this vision. After hearing the responses from pastors around the country, I knew the need was real; it was confirmed many times over.

There's a certain sacrifice that's required to birth a dream that you don't know about upfront. When you move from doing to being—to living and ministering out of who you are—you will be asked to make nonrational decisions, to trust God and be willing to do what seems counterintuitive or really risky and even stupid, but you know it's right.

After resigning from his role at the seminary, Randy went on to found a nonprofit called VantagePoint3. He is the president of VP3, an organization committed to deepening and empowering adults and grooming them toward the work of leadership in the local church. The spiritual formation and leadership development processes that Randy and his team have developed give participants a vantage point to consider three questions: Who is God? Who am I? and What does God want to do through me? Randy and Rob Loane, an associate at VP3, coauthored *Deep Mentoring: Guiding Others on their Leadership Journey.*

2

BROODING

Before I can tell my life what I want to do with it,
I must listen to my life telling me who I am.
I must listen for the truths and values at
the heart of my own identity, not the
standards by which I must live—but
the standards by which I cannot
help but live if I am
living my own life.

Herbert Alphonso

*A*N ARTIST FRIEND OF OURS STUMBLED onto a creative process when she simply started pouring paint onto a canvas. It was during a very painful time in her life, one she had no words to describe nor any way to get in touch with. So one day she bought some clearance paint at a store, brought it home and started pouring colors together. As the cool and bright tones combined and swirled, undirected but somehow purposeful, she stood over the canvas and studied what emerged. Deborah began to see images, shapes and words come to the surface and surrendered to them, adding her own flourishes.

The result was not only an extraordinary and beautiful work of art, but emotional healing from this therapeutic process. She described the effects of what happened when she gave herself to this new way: "An alternative universe began to emerge. I became a reverent but wounded observer, detached but willing to see a new design—still providential but unintended."

IN THE BEGINNING

Deborah's process is how I imagine the Spirit of God's creative process. "In the beginning God created the heavens and the earth. The earth was formless and empty, and darkness covered the deep waters. And the Spirit of God was hovering over the surface of the waters" (Genesis 1:1-2). *Hovering.* What exactly was the Spirit doing—hovering? I picture the Spirit brooding, deep in thought, trying to discern how to shape and form the earth according to the creative instincts stirring within the heart of the Trinity.

If you've ever been involved in any creative process, making art, cooking a new recipe, planning a worship experience or writing a book, you know that it's hard and messy work. You start with the raw materials and your own creative instincts, and then together things just start happening. And sometimes the outcome takes on a life of its own. That's fairly descriptive of what it's like to make initial sense of a dream.

A DESTINY EXPERIENCE

For Randy Reese there was a poignant moment when he began to make sense of this vision forming within him to help develop Christian leaders. He had just moved to California to attend Fuller Seminary. For some time Randy had been mulling over some observations and gut instincts he had about how to develop effective leaders within and for the church, and began to ask the question, Could there be an effective process to do this?

One day, as he was traveling on the 210 freeway, Randy had an experience with God. He'd been meditating on Ephesians 2:10 for some time: "We are what he has made us, created in Christ Jesus for good works, which God prepared beforehand to be our way of life" (NRSV). Suddenly, a clear thought came to mind that he sensed was from God: "I want to use you to deepen and empower the church in North America." He immediately felt a distinct blend of deep fear and deep joy as he considered this invitation.

> Because I'd been studying Christian leadership by one of Fuller's professors, J. Robert Clinton, I knew that the people God selected to do kingdom work often had a lot of destiny experiences. Clinton called them "awe inspiring" moments. So, one day, as I anticipated attending a luncheon for new doctoral students, and aware that I needed a Fuller faculty to sponsor me in the program, I prayed a specific prayer, "God, would you hook me up with Dr. Clinton so that I have a sponsor."
>
> I was late to lunch and there was only one seat left at a table in the back corner of the room. An elderly man stood up, said hello, and asked me to sit next to him. It was Robert Clinton. I told him what I'd prayed. He took that as a cue to invite me into his office after lunch. Later that afternoon, he said, "I think you need to study with me in the doctoral program."

Not all of us will have destiny moments as stunning and convincing as Randy's—though it's a beautiful thing when we do! There are other ways to gain confidence and make sense of the energy and ideas that are taking shape within us.

PAYING ATTENTION TO VALUES

When I began to pay attention in earnest to the dream within me, it felt formless, lacking substance, and the shape was unclear. I knew that I had a desire to start something new. I had some ideas of what that "new" might be—offering hospitality to others, creating a sacred space for conversations, modeling spiritual practices and offering spiritual direction. I had the colors I wanted to work with, but I didn't know what the shapes and images—what the picture—were to look like.

About that time, I worked through an exercise as part of a spiritual formation/leadership development process called "The Journey," a process that was written by Randy Reese and Rob Loane. It was an exercise to clarify my values—something I don't recall ever doing before. The material defined a value as "a deeply held belief that possesses the worth to influence decisions made and actions taken." The curriculum went on to say that values

> are the convictions that travel with us through life's challenges and opportunities. These deeply held beliefs act as guides for decision-making, steering us in our choices of how to do what we desire to do. They are matters of the heart that result in commitments. Sometimes we are conscious of these beliefs and other times we are not.

Discerning my values began to give me greater clarity about the dream in my heart, what I was to create.

Pause for a moment with me and let's return to the image of the Spirit hovering over the formless earth, about to explode with creative juices. What were the ideas stirring in the heart of God that led to the cosmos as we know it? Could it be that the Spirit put expression to the triune God's values? Considering that there were a myriad of creative options which could have been, the fact that our world is marked by beauty, organization, freedom, diversity, reproductivity and relationship, it seems that the Creator God was working from a template, a template of God's own personal values.

If values are deeply held beliefs that act as guides in our decisions and actions, then it makes sense that our values might be the raw material of a God-given dream. Values aren't simply personal preferences. Not really. If you get in touch with your real values and you reflect on where they come from, you will notice that God has likely instilled them in you through your life journey, through the shaping experiences of your life and your response to those experiences.

For instance, the value that came to the top of my list is my desire to live and invite others to a contemplative life, to have a pace and scope to my lifestyle that allows me time to be still and listen to God and my own heart. I know where that value comes from. As a young child, even though an extravert, I was drawn to and nourished by being alone in nature. This value of slowing down, of introverting, has a deep vein in me. As an adult, I have grown in cultivating a contemplative life—a life of deliberate thoughtfulness. I've learned how to live reflectively and I see the fruit of paying attention to my inner life. Because this goes against my extroverted personality, I know it's a value that has taken hold in me by God and through my life experiences.

As you are brooding over the deep waters of your own heart, paying attention to the shapes, images and words that surface, it may be helpful for you to work through a process of discerning your own personal values. The following exercise is adapted from "The Journey." (For more information about "The Journey," visit VP3's website at vantagepoint3.org.)

REFLECTION: DISCERNING YOUR PERSONAL VALUES

The following questions are not easy to answer. They will require time and reflection. The answers to the questions won't necessarily be automatic; we are not always conscious of our values, nor have we tried to put them into words or statements before. Something that can help is to sit down with a close friend, spouse, family member or spiritual director *after* you have come up with your own responses and ask the person to describe your values and then compare their answers with your own.

- What do you spend the most time doing?
- What do you spend the most time thinking about?
- What do you spend the most time talking about?
- Where do you find yourself giving the most effort or caring the most?
- What vexes you? Causes you the most anger or indignation?
- What excites you? Causes you the greatest joy and satisfaction?
- What do you find to be really important to you at this time in your life?

Now spend some time *prayerfully* brooding over your answers. What guiding values seem to come to the surface? Ask God to help you see what's important to see, and write down five to seven personal values. You could begin each statement with "I value . . ."

As you consider the values you have named, what more do you learn about this dream that may be taking shape and form within you?

INTERVIEW

Phileena Heuertz and Gravity—a Center
for Contemplative Activism

𝒯HE JOURNEY OF BECOMING YOUR TRUE SELF can be an arduous task, and there are some who engage in the task with tremendous tenacity and courage. Phileena Heuertz is one of those people. Growing up as the daughter of a pastor in a conservative and restrictive culture shaped her childhood identity around certain dos and don'ts—especially as a girl. But when Phileena came of age, this small and tightly bound self she had become began to feel suffocated, and she started to gasp for air.

Her awakening began in earnest after many years traveling with her husband, Chris, to some of the most despairing and difficult places in the world, caring for the most vulnerable—children, orphans and widows. Phileena and Chris were tired and needed rest. Soon after, they received the gift of an extended sabbath. During their sabbatical, they planned a thirty-three-day pilgrimage along the ancient path of El Camino de Santiago in Spain. Phileena described in hindsight what was happening inside her during that time:

> Months prior to setting out on the Camino, I had the sense that I would not be the same when I returned. In a state of awakening, my identity was being shaken and dismantled, and I was entering

an internal nakedness. It's difficult to describe this experience. Only in hindsight can I really name it for what it was. I felt like I was losing my orientation for life, relationships and service.

Losing one's orientation, being shaken and dismantled can feel like a disorienting undoing. Somehow, Phileena knew it was the only way forward and leaned into it with openness and curiosity. Drinking deeply of the quiet and ambled pace of her pilgrimage, Phileena began to open herself *to herself* and to God more fully. The dismantling of a tightly bound identity and the receiving or, rather, entering into a more expansive and expressive self began to happen in the space of a contemplative season. During this time, Phileena embraced the countermovement to an active life—contemplation, of slowing and receiving from God rather than incessant giving to God. She experienced the effect of a posture and environment that awakened her more fully to the woman God had created her to be.

Not long after, Phileena had an epiphany, a God moment when she welcomed an invitation to create an organization that would promote and empower God's people to hold in tension the movements of contemplation and activism; that vision became Gravity—a center for contemplative activism. Located in the heart of Omaha, Phileena and Chris welcome fellow pilgrims to journey with them as they explore how to be both activists seeking justice and healing for people in poverty, *and* contemplatives who draw near to God and receive healing and integration for themselves.

Phileena and Chris Heuertz founded Gravity after twenty years of grassroots work in some of the world's poorest slums, red light areas and places of intense human suffering. The Gravity Center exists to nurture the integral connection between social engagement and contemplative spirituality—to do good better. Gravity facilitates contemplative retreats, spiritual direction and pilgrimages to places of religious significance, as well as places marked by profound pain and hope. Phileena is the author of *Pilgrimage of a Soul: Contemplative Spirituality for the Active Life.*

3

WELCOMING

*Although it may be frightening to trust our desires, they are
always fundamentally spiritual. In fact, they are often
the most direct access we have to the subtle
movement of the Spirit within
our own spirits.*

David Benner

AS LONG AS I CAN REMEMBER, I've had a precarious relationship with my desires. For some reason, a reason I don't
fully understand, I've often doubted what I truly want; I've questioned
it—assumed that it was selfish or too much. Even as young as the age
of six I can remember making a regrettable decision to betray my true
wishes in favor of what seemed more reasonable.

It was my sixth birthday, and my grandma had offered to buy me a
brand new bedroom suite as a gift. I knew this was an expensive gift and
that she didn't have a lot of money. One Saturday morning she picked
me up and we drove to a furniture store in the small town where we lived.
As we meandered through the displays, looking at all our options, I finally
saw one that made me light up—a beautiful white, French provincial set
with scalloped edges painted in gold and a canopy bed. It was, without
question, the canopy that I loved most of all.

I watched the salesperson as she sat at a small table and began to write down each of the pieces that we chose, with the price next to them: this hutch, that chest of drawers, this nightstand. When we came to the canopy, my grandma turned to me and asked if I wanted it. I looked at it—probably an extra-long gaze—and turned to my grandma and said no.

She seemed puzzled and questioned me again. I repeated my answer, no.

Can you guess why I said no? Do you have a hunch about what was going on inside me that led me to say no to something that I really, *really* wanted? As I remember this experience, I recall a little voice inside tugging at my conscience, reminding me that "good little girls don't ask for too much." The canopy just seemed too much for me.

I don't know if you can relate to my story or not. I do know from many of my interviews with people who have embraced a God-given dream that it's not uncommon to feel some strong reservations to welcome that dream. A voice inside rises up in protest and questions, *Who do you think you are?* As David Benner suggests in the epigraph, we learn to distrust our desires; we assume that they are too much or too selfish to admit to ourselves, let alone anyone else. And yet *what if our desires are the most direct access to the subtle work of the Spirit within us?*

AMBIVALENCE

As Phileena Heuertz began to recognize a dream growing within her to found the Gravity Center, her initial response was one of noticeable and confusing ambivalence.

I was visiting with some dear friends from India who were living in San Francisco and expecting their second child. My life at that point was very full and intense, but I was away from all of that. They lived in an apartment, and behind it was this lovely lagoon. I'm really drawn to water. One day, as I'm walking around this lagoon, all of a sudden I had this overwhelming sense that my life was about to change, that I was going to be creating a sacred space for people to come and retreat, and it was going to demand my full-time attention.

It was more of a feeling than a thought, an overwhelming sense of presence, hope, delight, anticipation and freedom. In that moment, I was "full with this thing"—not knowing what it would look like, where or how it would come to be.

And then, almost immediately, I was overcome with anxiety—major anxiety. Life was great, and all of sudden I was no longer content with things as they were. But I didn't know what was coming. It was a "get ready" moment. Something's coming, and it's going to be different.

I can relate to Phileena's sense of fullness and being overwhelmed by it all at the same time. When I began to take my dream seriously, I experienced my own internal protests. I felt inadequate and foolish to think that this idea could ever become a reality through my efforts. I wrote in my journal: "I don't know what to do with this dream. It, frankly, seems so 'out there,' beyond me and impossible." I felt nervous to tell anyone other than David. Sometimes I talked about it in generalities, but couldn't muster the confidence to speak up and say, "Here it is! And I'm gonna do this." And so I kept it to myself for a long time.

YOU CAN'T MEAN ME?

I wonder what kind of inner voices Mary, the mother of Jesus, heard inside her head when she pondered the news that she'd been chosen to give birth to the Son of God, Israel's Messiah. I don't know how well you know her story, but she was probably only thirteen or fourteen at the time, inexperienced in life, let alone motherhood. She was young, naive, innocent Mary.

Then an angel showed up one day and said, "Greetings, favored woman! The Lord is with you!" (Luke 1:28). She had to have felt flustered by his introduction. Maybe she thought to herself, *You can't mean me!* And then Gabriel told her the news that she would conceive and give birth to a son, the Son of the Most High, and he would reign over Israel forever. How do you welcome *that* kind of news? How do you tell your family and friends, let alone your fiancé, something that seems both miraculous and ridiculous?!

A WALL OF RESISTANCE

When we begin to pay serious attention to a budding dream within us, at some point we may meet a wall of resistance that comes in some form of self-doubt. *Am I really the person to do this? Do I have the qualifications to pull it off? Where's this idea coming from anyway?* These questions expose our feelings of inadequacy and the fear that if we told anyone about our idea, he or she would seriously question our judgment or laugh in our face.

So, what do we do with a dream that's tangled up in feelings of inadequacy and insecurity?

I want to look again at Mary's story, but before I do, let me add a caveat: it's important not to turn her or any biblical character into a superhero. I'm sure she had her moments of self-doubt and mornings of upset stomachs that weren't just morning sickness. Yet her response was quite remarkable. She answered Gabriel, "I am the Lord's servant. May everything you have said about me come true" (Luke 1:38). How do you describe her incredible comeback? Consenting? Yielding? Welcoming?

To me, it was like Mary greeted this news as an unexpected visitor knocking on her door. She opened the door and said, "Welcome," received the news with hospitality, determined to be its servant. She exuded an unspoken trust in God to provide what she needed to care for this startling caller.

So, how did she do that? I don't know. Was it naivety or youthful idealism that fueled her swift response? Or was it a deep faith in God and, perhaps, a learned habit—a spiritual practice—of obedient surrender? Perhaps it was all of the above, all mixed together.

Phileena also had a mixture of feelings and responses to her overwhelming sense that life was about to change. Immediately, after she became "full with this thing," she felt significant anxiety to the point that she couldn't sleep. For several weeks, in fact, she struggled with insomnia, which only compounded her anxiety.

Phileena explained,

> Psychologically, I was preparing for change without having all the answers for how things would be different. Simultaneously, I was longing for this new thing in my life that was little more than a spark, an intuition, a far-off dream, and worried and anxious about the changes it would demand. It took months for my mind and emotions to stabilize. That was 2011. It was a couple of months later that I spoke at the Q Conference on contemplative spirituality. It was my coming out. I had the sense that this was an important message for the church. From that point on, I began to receive more invitations to speak and the Gravity Center started to take shape and form.

Phileena spoke to me about how her anxiety stemmed, in part, from the invitation to develop greater trust in herself. "That felt overwhelming." God was asking her to take on larger responsibility and leadership, which conflicted with the voice of her background, of a patriarchal culture where women were restricted to play only certain roles, and always in submission to men. Like my "good little girls don't ask for too much" motto, Phileena confronted a voice of incrimination. Over time, she mustered the courage to face it, press through it and eventually welcome her visitor. Be it unto *me* as you have said.

If, or more likely when, you hit this wall of resistance, you may wonder how to work through your ambivalence at opening the door to this "stranger." The following reflection is a process to help you consciously and intentionally welcome your dream.

REFLECTION: WELCOMING YOUR DREAM

- Read Luke 1:26-38 a few times slowly and intently. What do you notice? Where is your attention drawn?

- How would you feel if you were Mary?

- Do you have some of the same feelings as you consider welcoming your dream? How would you describe them?

- What insecurities or feelings of inadequacy are stirred up as you contemplate realizing your dream?

- Where do those voices of doubt come from? Do you know about their origin?

- If you were to name one thing that is holding you back from welcoming your dream, what would it be?

- How might you bring these things to God in prayer?

- Mary responded to God, "May everything you have said about *me* come true." Are you ready to make these words your prayer? If so, pause and express them to God.

- Now consider identifying a few people you would like to share your dream with. Remember to be careful who you choose. Sharing your dream with someone who is prone to be critical or even too practical can be a demoralizing experience and cause a setback in your confidence and courage.

- Take initiative to share with them what you're thinking. Ask them to help you by praying for you.

INTERVIEW

Chris Smith and the Englewood Review of Books

*S*OME OF THE DREAMS WE SHAPE and the dreams that shape us are related primarily to our vocation, some are related to the way we live our lives, and some are related to both. Chris Smith's life and vocation have become a unified expression of how he lives out his God-given dream. As a young boy Chris grew up in Maryland, in a bedroom community outside Washington, D.C., where life moved fast and neighbors led private, isolated lives. In contrast, however, some of his childhood days were punctuated by a hiatus to a quieter, more connected life when he visited his mother's siblings who lived in Mennonite communities in Iowa and Ohio. What Chris experienced of life in those communities—a simpler, smaller, rooted life—left a strong impression on him; it appealed to him and began to shape his desires into adulthood.

Many years later, Chris entered graduate school at Indiana University. At that point in time he pictured himself heading toward a life of teaching and writing in the context of higher education. During his first year, he had a fellowship that went well and helped give focus to his studies. But during his second year, things began to change. Chris had an assistantship, and the intensity of his work soon began to burn him out. In addition, Chris's research was abstract—the history and philosophy of geometry. (Yeah, try to wrap your mind around that.) His academic work felt isolating, and he felt very alone. It was a low point in his life, one from which he needed a break.

At the same time that he was feeling burned out from academia, Chris was also experiencing a growing desire to live in community with others. Soon to be married, Chris decided to take a leave of absence from grad school. Once married, he and Jeni moved to Cincinnati to be interns at Community House, an intentional community. Over the course of the year the dream of being an academic died a quiet death.

Chris didn't know what was ahead; he had had such an intense experience of burnout and the self-absorption of academic life that he knew he couldn't go back. For him the burden and desire for community could not coexist with the demands of a vocation in higher education. So, after a year in Cincinnati, he and Jeni moved to Indianapolis and began to search for the kind of community and vocation they wanted to characterize their life. Chris explains,

> So we were trying to figure out what this meant—this idea of living intentionally in community. There's a passage from Bonhoeffer's book *Life Together* where he talks about the visionary dreamer whose vision of community is more important than the actual community. We had to die to the abstract idea of community in order to live into the "real" community we were looking for. It takes time to shape a dream so that it can become what God intends.

Eventually, Chris and Jeni found the community their hearts yearned for and soon became part of Englewood Christian Church. Englewood folks are intentional and interdependent in the way they live as a community and have a vision to "bring the Kingdom of God to life" through their collective presence in their neighborhood on the Near Eastside of Indianapolis. They see their community as the focal point where the dreams of individuals and their "place" come together. Englewood hopes to embody Christ in and through their local congregation as they discern and grow deeper and more mature in ways that are attentive to the work of the kingdom.

Through Chris's involvement with Englewood and the Englewood Community Development Corporation, he also discovered a compatible vocation—one that he said, in a lot of ways, feels like a return to his original academic dream. In 2007 Chris, with the discernment and support of his community, founded the *Englewood Review of Books*. Chris is the editor of this weekly online review and quarterly print magazine, which features resources for the people of God as they follow the mission of God. The books reviewed are not necessarily books from the mainstream Christian market, and many aren't found in your local Christian bookstore. For those who love to read, Chris offers a very interesting and eclectic mix of book reviews along with his own thoughtful musings. Chris not only reviews books, he writes them as well. He, along with John Pattison, recently authored *Slow Church: Cultivating Community in the Patient Way of Jesus.*

4

DISCERNING

The crossroads of change and choice can be a very confusing place.
At times a fog rolls in and obscures our vision. We feel paralyzed,
exhausted, frightened, alone. Our hopes are shattered. Instead of
being able to look down various paths, we can scarcely see
our own feet, much less a path. Our ability to think is
constricted. Our energy is limited. The process
of discernment is overthrown as we
concentrate on just surviving.

Lois A. Lindbloom

HE GOD I'VE COME TO KNOW over my adult life is a God who is more interested in the formation of my personhood than my personal comfort. He's more interested in who I am than the outcome or achievements of my life. His concern is whether, through the circumstances of my life, I'm becoming more like Jesus as I become my true self."

I found this entry in my journal as I was reflecting on the last several years of birthing Sustainable Faith Indy. I wrote it at a time when I wasn't especially happy about God's commitment to my personhood. We'd come a long way from the beginning of this story where I had a vague, unnamable dream in my heart. We'd come a long way from David being *for me* but not *with me*. But at the point when I wrote this, we were stalled. Our house had been on the market several months, properties that we'd fallen in love with had sold, and we sat, waiting and wondering if what I'd conjured up as a dream was really a pipe dream.

The demanding journey of bringing a dream to life requires persistent courage and conviction because the path forward can be convoluted and the process confusing. In the midst of the milieu an important question often emerges: Is this dream *really from God* and *for me*?

This is a big question and requires thoughtful discernment.

For me, the discernment process didn't follow a straightforward line. I would like to tell you that it came together in a sincere moment of prayer when light dawned and I knew beyond a shadow of a doubt that God wanted me to do this thing. And then magically the stars aligned and everything fell in to place to confirm God's blessed approval. Hardly.

What the discernment process became for me was a long, circuitous path of yearning, seeking, confusion and waiting as the longing I experienced and the challenges I faced exposed what was in my heart. My responses to the process became the content of agonizing and honest prayer, where I met God in the depths of my being and sought to know his will for me.

- I wrestled in prayer with my mixture of motives. Some seemed to be pure, from and for God, and others seemed to be out of self-serving desire.

- I wrestled in prayer with the nature of my energy for this dream. Sometimes I felt free, like I was being drawn toward it, and other times I felt anxiously and compulsively driven.

- I wrestled in prayer with what might be false assumptions versus real faith. Was it right to assume that the life I was being drawn toward would be more satisfying and in line with who I am, or was I fooling myself that the grass was going to be greener on the other side of this dream?

LOOKING FOR TOUCHSTONES

Through entering into prayer with this conglomerate of motives, energies and beliefs, God began to purify my desires and instill deep hope. Though I waited a long time before my desires became a living reality, eventually God forged in me the confidence that this dream was indeed from him and for me. I wrote in my journal toward the end of the process, though at the time, I didn't know I was close to the end:

> What is giving me a touchstone of love or guidance in my current situation? [A question asked by Lois Lindbloom in *Cultivating Discernment in Spiritual Direction*.]
>
> As I sit with this question, I am aware of the hope I feel in my heart. Despite the fact that there have been delays and lots of uncertainty related to our move, I continue to feel hope within me. I keep looking for God, entrusting our lives and this big move to him. I think that God, the Spirit, is the hope. His companionship is the hope. I'm reminded of Romans 5:3-5: "We can rejoice, too, when we run into problems and trials, for we know that they help us develop endurance. And endurance develops strength of character, and character strengthens our confident hope of salvation. And this hope will not lead to disappointment. For we know how dearly God loves us, because he has given us the Holy Spirit to fill our hearts with his love." Whatever God does, he does in love.

Sometimes the rugged, uphill grade of the path toward realizing a dream exposes the content of our hearts and can purify our desires. Through it, we are reminded of God's greater concern for who we are becoming rather than what we are doing for him. He seems to take the long way around the block because he has so much more on his mind than just putting us where he wants us, so he can do great things through us, or, more honestly, we can do great things for him. He cares about the kind of people we are because only when we are *real* people do we have something to offer the world.

So, I hope you will take this to heart as you begin working on your dream. If you don't find things falling into place, coming together effortlessly, don't assume that this is an indication you are misguided in your discernment of God's will. On the contrary, the birthing process is erratic and labor intensive, and it is through the challenges we face and our response to those challenges that God provides the confirmation we need.

While you are paying attention to this dream developing within you, I encourage you to also pay attention to the deeper work God is doing in your inner life and character. When it's all said and done, if you can find amid the rubble any shards of pure, clean desire and enduring hope, then you may have discovered the confirmation you are looking for.

REFLECTION: A PERSONAL AND PRAYERFUL APPROACH TO DISCERNMENT

- Describe what you are noticing in your responses and reactions to the process of giving birth to your dream.

- Describe what you notice about yourself and your motives.

- How would you describe your energy for this dream? What does the energy feel like?

- What assumptions do you have about realizing this dream that you wonder are true or false?

- As you prayerfully reflect on your internal attitudes toward birthing your dream, can you identify what seems like pure desire and enduring hope? Describe what you see.

- How are or aren't you experiencing God through this process?

DISCERNMENT IN COMMUNITY

I have been illustrating personal discernment that happens in prayer. There is great value, however, in inviting others into discernment with you. That's what Chris Smith shared as his experience when we talked about his dream.

The positive impression that Mennonite communities had on Chris when he visited them as a young boy never left him. A seed was planted in his young heart that grew into a conscious desire and pursuit in his adult life. So when he and his wife, Jeni, moved to Indianapolis, it made sense that they would find many kindred spirits at Englewood Christian Church. Englewood folks approach being church and doing community very differently from most churches around. And one of the ways they function uniquely is in how they help "discern and refine where the dreams of the individual meet the mission of God through the people of God in their local community."

Early on, Chris joined the staff of the Englewood Community Development Corporation (ECDC). He explains,

> I'd been on staff with the Englewood Community Development Corporation that had been started by the church. But most of my income came through selling used books. I've always loved books. I started selling and collecting them in college.
>
> My salary was covered by selling used books, but during the recession of 2007 I lost about three-fourths of my income. So, our community asked, What do we do? We came to the idea of doing the *Englewood Review of Books*. Our community discernment started with the folks who worked closely with ECDC. It started there, but once we refined it and realized that this was possible, we took it to the church's ministry council. Part of the process was asking questions and pushing back.
>
> We knew we wouldn't make a lot of money doing book reviews, but it was in line with the publishing and book selling we were already doing, and so we pooled our email address list and had about one hundred people we sent a review to every Friday. People loved it! We launched a website six months later. Today we have about four thousand subscribers. I honestly don't remember who

suggested the idea of publishing book reviews. But once the idea was put out there, it made sense. I don't think I would have ever come to it if Englewood wasn't the sort of church community that pointed me in that direction and had the business structure to help.

REFLECTION: CALLING A CLEARNESS COMMITTEE

About the time that David and I were ready to give up on our dream, we asked our community, a small group that we'd been a part of for four years, to sit with us and help us listen to what God was saying to us. They agreed, and through the simple format of a Quaker practice called a "Clearness Committee," we received some important questions to consider and greater clarity related to our dilemma and need for discernment.

What follows is an adapted version of the clearness committee process as described by author and educator Parker Palmer. You might consider using this process, when the time is right, to invite others' help in discerning whether this dream inside you is from God and for you to tend.

Many of us face a dilemma when trying to deal with a personal problem, question, or decision. On the one hand, we know that the issue is ours alone to resolve and that we have the inner resources to resolve it, but access to our own resources is often blocked by layers of inner "stuff"—confusion, habitual thinking, fear, despair. On the other hand, we know that friends might help us uncover our inner resources and find our way, but by exposing our problem to others, we run the risk of being invaded and overwhelmed by their assumptions, judgments, and advice—a common and alienating experience. As a result, we often privatize these vital questions in our lives: at the very moment when we need all the help we can get, we find ourselves cut off from both our inner resources and the support of a community.

For people who have experienced this dilemma, I want to describe a method invented by the Quakers, a method that protects individual identity and integrity while drawing on the wisdom of other people. It is called a "Clearness Committee."

I have adapted the following steps that Palmer suggests. For the complete article, see "The Clearness Committee" at couragerenewal.org/parker /writings/clearness-committee.

1. Select a group of people you trust to assist you in this discernment process. I would recommend a minimum of three and no more than eight.

2. Before meeting, take time to reflect and write a concise statement of the issue you're trying to resolve, provide relevant background information and offer any hunches on what you think is happening. Provide this to each of your Clearness Committee participants.

3. The meeting typically lasts two hours; designate (ahead of time) one person to facilitate the meeting and another person to take notes.

4. The time begins when you break the silence and share briefly about your situation, what's going on and how you are feeling about it.

5. The participants then respond, but only with open, honest questions. This is imperative! An open, honest question is one where the asker can't predict the answer. The questions should help *you* be curious about some aspect of your situation.

6. You are invited to respond to each question that feels of value to you. You get to decide. Take time and give full explanations, without sharing your whole life story or information that isn't pertinent.

7. As you respond, the participants will think of additional questions and can ask them in order to drill down deeper into the subject matter. They should be asked in a slow, gentle, unforced way.

8. Fifteen minutes before it's time to end, if you desire, invite the participants to mirror back to you what they've heard you say. Again, they mirror but don't offer advice.

9. Keep in mind that you may not have your answer(s) by the end of the time. What you have will continue to stew in you for some time, eventually providing the clarity and confidence you need to either lay the dream down or pick it up and move forward.

Part Two

SHAPING A
GOD-GIVEN DREAM

INTERVIEW

MaryBeth Jackson and the Viewfinder Project

*M*ARYBETH JACKSON UNDERSTANDS MORE clearly now what she's intuitively known for a long time—that the way we look at the world affects how we see it, respond to it and live in it. People are empowered to change the world when they change the way they see their world. Like the French novelist Marcel Proust suggested, "The true voyage of discovery exists not in seeking new landscapes but in having new eyes."

MaryBeth traces the origin of her God-given dream all the way back to her sixteenth birthday, when she asked for a camera and photography lessons. Instantly, she bonded with what became an appendage of her "new eyes" and started photographing the world around her. "I took my first photography class when I was sixteen. I loved it! I proceeded to sign up for any photography class I could during high school. Every class was hyperfocused on the elements of photography. I began to notice things I'd never noticed before."

MaryBeth's love of photography continued to influence her throughout college and on to graduate school, where she studied communications, culture and technology, with an emphasis on children and media. "In this media-saturated country of ours, I was really concerned with how kids were being impacted. On the day I defended my thesis, my adviser asked me a formative question: 'How do you make the kids the content producers of the media?'"

That question stayed with MaryBeth and primed the pump of her imagination about how to involve kids in the creative process, and what might happen to the way they see things if they were involved. Not long after, she and Kyle, her husband, traveled to South Africa, and she found herself thinking one day:

I wonder what is ugly to the kids here? And I wonder what is beautiful? What if I gave them cameras—what would they photograph?

So, using a translator, I met with some middle-school-aged kids over the course of three days and handed them disposable cameras. These kids had never held cameras before. I asked the kids to take pictures of anything that they thought was ugly and anything they thought was beautiful. They came back in ten minutes. I had allocated thirty. I thought to myself, *They didn't get it.* Then I developed the film and discovered, *They did get it!*

I found *beautiful* pictures of trash, rotting wood, rusty cars and broken windows, and beautiful pictures of grandmothers, flowers, self-portraits and a pretty door. When they were finished, the headmaster said, "The kids loved this! Do you have anything else?"

So, I went home and wrote eleven more lessons. That's when all my photography classes came back to me, and the name for this project came together as well.

MaryBeth incorporated the Viewfinder Project in 2007—a nonprofit that uses photography to help middle school-aged kids "see life differently." Through the curriculum that MaryBeth has written, approximately 2,500 children and adults in fifteen countries have been equipped to become change makers in their communities—through learning to see life with new eyes.

The Viewfinder Project currently comprises sixteen lesson plans that can be implemented by anyone who believes that beauty can be found in anything. The lessons are written for students of 10-14 years, but can be and have been utilized by people of all ages. Hope and creativity is fostered when kids and adults gain the ability to focus on what is good and beautiful in the world and that is what inspires change.

5

NAMING

All enterprises or projects, big or small, begin in the mind's eye;
they begin with imagination and with the belief that
what's merely an image can one day be made real.

Jim Kouzes and Barry Posner

WHEN A COUPLE DISCOVER THAT THEY ARE expecting a baby, the idea that a tangible, living being now exists as a byproduct of their procreation can feel pretty elusive at first. Even as a mother's belly swells and the father feels with his hands a protruding elbow or kicking foot, the baby can still be hard to imagine. But then something happens—almost magically—when this couple chooses a name. As seemingly nonsubstantive as a name might appear, when they can call their baby by name, that baby becomes someone.

The same happens for people who are giving birth to a dream. The enterprise or project that has begun in your mind's eye, in your imagination, as Kouzes and Posner put it, may right now be just an idea—something that you believe in. But once you give it a name, it will begin to feel more real. When you can call it by name and talk about it using its name, it suddenly feels like it has substance and is becoming a reality. You may be ready to choose a name for your dream or have already chosen one. What's important here is to choose a name that will be enduring, that reflects the nature of your vision and feels comfortable to you when you speak it.

This is as significant a step in the process of birthing your dream as it was for MaryBeth Jackson when she, after many years of having a dream in the making, was able to name "her baby" the Viewfinder Project.

HAVING NEW EYES

"My whole pursuit of beauty has changed me," Mary Beth explained as she described what precipitated starting the Viewfinder Project. She had moved to Indianapolis from Oregon to marry her husband and began to feel a low-level depression because of the flat terrain, gray winters and stark cold. Having been overcome by the beauty of Portland and struggling to see it in Indiana was troubling to her. So, she started looking intentionally for what she'd experienced before; MaryBeth looked for "thin places." A thin place, originating from the Celtic Christian tradition, refers to where the veil between this world and the eternal world is thin.

> Portland was a "thin place" for me, a concept I connected with there, just not in Indiana. My husband would point out the simple beauty of native wildflowers, a flock of ducklings or beavers skimming the river's surface. I started to see the simple beauty around me, realizing beauty is not only in the majestic mountains and rivers of Oregon but also in the small things.

And that's when the pursuit of beauty changed her. MaryBeth discovered what she'd always known, that beauty is everywhere if you have eyes to see it!

When MaryBeth started the Viewfinder Project, she did so because of her belief and experience that what we choose to focus on affects how we see our world and respond to it. So, the first time she taught the kids in South Africa about photography and how to use a camera, she showed them how to focus their attention by making a viewfinder with their hands.

The idea here was that when taking a photo, you have to choose what you are going to capture, what view you are going to limit yourself to. I think I said, "If you could only look at the world through this little square, what would you focus on?" At the end of our time together, I took photos of each of the kids who participated. They all were making variations of some symbol with their hands, which I didn't recognize immediately. When I asked my husband what he thought they were doing, he said, "They're making a viewfinder, like you taught them!"

When MaryBeth began thinking about launching an organization and wondered what she should call it, she remembered those early photos of the kids and decided to call it the Viewfinder Project.

The name has come to simply represent the most basic parts of the camera, capturing your "view." But whenever I teach, I still always show the viewfinder with my hands and ask students to consider how they would focus their view if this was their window. Choosing what to focus on with the camera is a wonderful metaphor for life, one that is integral to the project and to the name.

Not all names for dreams come together as easily as this one did for MaryBeth. Whether or not the name for your dream surfaces effortlessly or with difficulty, hold out until you find one that captures the essence of your dream.

MAKING IT REAL

So, landing on a name can make the idea of your dream seem more real. But when you begin the naming process, sometimes you have to give a potential name a test drive. For instance, I toyed with several names for our urban retreat center. The first real name I considered was "the Greenhouse." I love gardening and liked the sound of this as well as the connotations of warmth and light and growth. But then I decided on a more descriptive name, which became, after a few iterations, the Center for

Contemplative Living. I still like that. I even owned that domain name for a while. You might say I took that name for a more serious test drive.

When I began to consider the name Sustainable Faith Indy, however, it was because of a dawning thought that perhaps Dave and Jody Nixon, founders of Sustainable Faith in Cincinnati, might be willing to partner with us in giving birth to our dream. I journaled about this, musing about the benefits of a partnership; I reasoned that it could provide increased credibility and helpful support—things that would be great benefits to a fledgling ministry like ours. I even recall drafting the email, with sweaty palms, asking Dave and Jody if they would consider what felt like a bold and presumptuous request. They responded quickly and with enthusiasm.

REFLECTION: CHOOSING A NAME

Choosing a name for your dream is a big deal. Yes, it might take time and a few attempts before you feel settled on where you have landed. A name is tied closely to your brand—that which distinguishes your dream from another's similar dream. Good names are integral to good brands and accomplish a number of things in promoting your dream. You want your name to be like a fragrance—one that gives off a memorable and distinctive scent.

The following are a few criteria to keep in mind as you think about names for your God-given dream.

- *It's important that your name represents your values.* Names have a personality. They reflect what you care deeply about. Like the View-finder Project, a name can say what your dream is about, both literally and philosophically. As you brainstorm possible names, look over your values and notice the language you use to describe them. Do you find any among those you identified that seem nameworthy? Begin a list.

- *It's important that your name connects emotionally with the people you want to reach.* The name you choose will hopefully speak to the heart of those who are "your people" if it conveys the right emotional vibe. Think about what you want people to feel and what associations you want them to make related to the names you are considering. For us, we believed the word sustainable would strike a chord with those looking for what we offer. We also felt that being associated with Sustainable Faith in Cincinnati was a positive thing.

- *Simple names are often more memorable.* Consider names that are simple and short enough to remember and to use in a link to your website or for your email address. Also, is there an abbreviation that you could use? We often refer to Sustainable Faith Indy as SFI or SF Indy.

- *Trendy names are typically regrettable.* As much as I liked the Green-house, I wondered how I would feel about it in ten years. Maybe I would still love it. It's a bit of a judgment call. But when you're looking over your list of names, ask yourself how each name would sound a decade from now. Is there a quality of timelessness about it?

- *Is the domain name taken?* One last thing that you will want to con-sider before you choose the name: make sure you can buy the domain name for your website (if you plan to have a website). To find out, visit Hover.com or Go Daddy and search to see if the domain name is available.

After you feel confident with the name you've chosen, or maybe have narrowed it down to two or three, run it by the kinds of people you hope will be drawn to and benefit from what you want to offer. Get their feedback. Ask them what associations they make with the name, what they think it describes. If they get a good vibe—that's confir-mation that you've found a good name that will accomplish what you hoped it would.

Once you've settled on a name, start using it in conversations and written communication. The more you get used to saying the name, the more real your dream will feel to you. As you talk about it, call your dream by name and begin to explain it to people. Explore words and phrases that feel energizing to you and capture your passion for your vision. Write them down so you don't forget them. Brand consistency is an important feature of getting across what you hope to create. These phrases and sentences will come in handy because the next step in this gestational process is writing a plan.

Take a deep breath. You can do it.

INTERVIEW

Elizabeth Roney and Liz Alig Fashion

WHEN ELIZABETH RONEY BEGAN TO STUDY the tags on clothing before she purchased them, she knew that something had changed. Through her travels around the world and exposure to the kinds of people who manufacture much of the apparel for the West, Liz began to see faces behind the clothes she bought. One particular scene was especially haunting. While visiting Nairobi, Kenya, Liz saw an old man sitting on top of a pile of tires, hand sewing shoes made out of the tires. Although she had seen similar scenes before, for some reason this one jarred her conscience more than others. And that's what changed her: first a face, then a conviction.

This experience became a catalyst for Liz to begin to pursue her God-given dream. In our interview, she gave me a little back story:

Six months after college, I did a bunch of things I didn't like, and they made me think *What do I really want to do?* I wanted to mix my interest overseas with fashion design. I had studied fashion design in Vienna during college, then had an internship in Africa, then took a trip to India after college for two months.

I didn't all at once think of it. I wanted to do something with fair trade, but when I started looking for fair trade fabric, I couldn't find any. About the same time, I went to a Goodwill Outlet where you buy fabric by the pound. I was so amazed at the amount of clothing that could be reused. I would find this really great fabric, an old curtain or something, and completely remake it into something else. *Wow! This is totally possible.* Then I gave them to some stores, and they sold.

Liz was probably as surprised as anyone that she could use upcycled textiles—from Goodwill no less—and remake them into stylish fashions and sell them to boutique owners for a profit. But that's exactly what she did! *And then she hit a snag.*

I had gotten to the point where I realized I couldn't sew all of the clothes myself and make a profit. I wasn't sure what to do. Over the summer, I went to Honduras and worked with a non-government organization (NGO) called Mi Esperanza. They were helping women out of poverty by teaching them to sew. While I was there, unrest in the country forced me to cut my trip short. With extra time on my hands, I got more serious about actually making a business plan. A few months later—when I needed help sewing— I asked Mi Esperanza to make a few dresses for me to see how it would go. This was the first time I produced in another country.

That was the beginning of Liz's partnership with other fair trade manufacturers around the world. She now works with co-ops and production facilities in Honduras, El Salvador, Guatemala, Ghana, India, Cambodia, Bangladesh, Nepal and the United States. Her clothing is vintage inspired with little added design details, including, and especially, pockets— her absolute favorite thing. Liz works as the design head from a small studio in Indianapolis and is dedicated to creating clothing that is both fashion forward and ethical.

6

SHAPING

The work which I do does not make me into the person I am;
rather the person who I am makes the work.

Martin Luther

N GENESIS 2, WHEN GOD LEANED OVER and scooped up mud with his hands and began to shape and form it into the first man, Adam, what kind of plan was he working with? What ideas did God have in his mind's eye as he pushed the clay between his palms, flattened it with his fingers, molded it, studied it and fashioned it some more?

How long did it take God to complete his work and stop fiddling? When he was done, did the man look like he'd imagined? Were there any surprises? And what about the moment when God leaned over this lifeless shape and breathed his breath into Adam. How long was it before Adam sputtered his first breath; how long before his flesh warmed with life and his heart pumped and his blood pulsated? What was it like for God to see his creation alive—taking his first independent breaths and steps?

Then at some point God saw the need for an adjustment to his plan. It wouldn't do to have Adam be alone. Once again, God used his hands to take from Adam's sleeping body a section of rib and to mold and make it into Eve. Now there were two, each created in God's image, created for each other.

At this point, I imagine God's heart full—very full—as he stepped back and saw the culmination of his dream before him. In fact, I'm pretty sure God was giddy with delight that what he had envisioned in his mind and worked so hard to create had in reality come to be. Fancy that!

The progression that I've just described—through my own imagination—of God's creative process is similar to ours. We start with the raw material of an idea we have and we start forming and shaping it between the folds of gray matter in our brain. We have a picture in mind that we're working from, one that goes through several adaptations before we feel fairly certain we have it.

And then the moment comes when we name it and breathe life into it, and it comes to be! We step back, look at it and feel surprised at how it's turned out—that it turned out. There are calluses on our hands and wrinkles on our brow to prove it's taken work. And that work isn't over. We may still have adjustments to make. But like God, we are giddy, our hearts full, as we watch in amazement at the work of our hands.

Luther said, "The work which I do does not make me into the person I am; rather the person who I am makes the work." What an important reminder as we consider the shaping of our dream. Just as the personality of God shaped the work of his creation, so the work that we give our hands to will be, and should be, marked by our unique personhood.

FROM A HOBBY TO A BUSINESS

When you browse the Liz Alig website, it's obvious that the person—Liz—has shaped the work she does. Her values of caring for the faces behind clothing manufacturing and her sensibilities for unique and fashionable style merge together in her clothing line. But for Liz, the real stretch came when she went from her dream being a hobby to it becoming a business. When she left Honduras because of the coup and returned to the United States, Liz started working on a business plan.

Putting a structure to her vision and developing it into a commercial enterprise was the biggest challenge yet.

In her own words,

> I'm not really a natural business or financial person. I still don't think I do it well, but I'm just doing it anyway. I'm asking questions, talking to friends, to people who own businesses. I never really pictured myself having a business, especially this young. Sometimes I still wonder how I got here. It's a lot of work. I've had to learn to separate myself from my dream. Realizing why I'm doing it is what keeps me going.

So Liz developed a business plan—albeit a rough first draft. She dug in and learned with each step how to shape and develop her business. Liz would admit it was scary, especially because it required taking risks even when she lacked the confidence and certainty that the risk would turn out well. Take for instance a trade show in Chicago where she paid $1,000 to display her clothing line. That was a lot of money to shell out on the long shot that some boutique owner would be interested in buying clothes made from upcycled fabric.

Liz recalled, "I didn't know how it would go. I was scared to death. And then I sold orders and made a profit! It all felt confirming because it was working. I just had to be willing to try things."

PUTTING FLESH ON THE BONES

Up to this point, tending your God-given dream has been a fairly creative and intuitive process. Now it's time to put some flesh on the bones, to begin capturing more clearly and in detail what it is that you want to create. Whether you use a template for a formal plan or work through the informal process that follows, it's up to you and the type of dream you have. What does matter is that you think, very concretely, about several important aspects of realizing a dream. But in the midst of working on the cerebral side of this process, don't forget to let your unique personality and heart shape the work.

When I got to this point, I felt anxious and overwhelmed with the idea of writing a business plan—the kind of plan that felt most appropriate to my dream. I'd never done anything like that before. And yet because my dream had a business side, it was important for me to take on this task. To bolster my confidence, I talked to several people who were knowledgeable about this kind of thing, people who had done something similar to what I wanted to do. I also searched the Internet to see what examples I could find. Between those two sources, I found a template that helped me capture my dream in one document.

Working through this was extremely helpful. It gave me the structure I needed to come up with my "elevator speech"—that concise and catchy version of what you say when someone asks what you're doing. This document is also helpful if your dream involves applying for nonprofit status or if you want to find investors or donors to contribute to your work. Let me share some of the important broad categories that you will need to flesh out your plan in written form and help you put skin on your dream.

Keep in mind, this is a working document and it will continue to evolve over the course of the time that it takes for you to begin implementing your dream. Even after that point, you will make adjustments to your plan. For right now, here is some direction to collect your ideas and record the details of how to organize your dream. Within each section is an important question for you to answer.

REFLECTION: SHAPING YOUR DREAM

- *Purpose.* The purpose defines the focus of the dream; it can include who this dream benefits and how they will benefit. For instance, I defined the purpose of Sustainable Faith Indy as an urban retreat center that would provide hallowed space for people to be still, pray, listen, process with others, learn and receive spiritual guidance.

  Question. What do you understand to be the purpose of your dream? Who does it serve? For what purpose? What do you hope to accomplish?

- *Need.* Often our dream is in response to a need we identify and feel motivated to meet. The need often names a personal passion; it flows from a deep conviction or value. (You might want to return to the values exercise [chap. 2] and see if it helps you define the need you are responding to.) The need that I identified was for people to live a more contemplative life, to slow down and consider the trajectory of their lives and their deeper longings.

Question. What needs in the world do you notice and see? What needs in the world most need to be met by you?

- *Scope or size.* The scope and size refers to how many people, communities, cities, countries (or issues) you hope to serve or shape.

  Question. What is the scope or size of your dream? Do you want to reach or influence the world, a region of the world or your local setting? What size groups of people do you want to serve?

- *Setting.* The setting describes where your dream will be realized. For example, I knew I was looking for a property in an urban neighborhood of Indianapolis, preferably a home that was around one hundred years old and had a stately, sacred feel. It also needed to be situated in a relatively quiet setting with adequate parking.

  Question. What is the setting where you hope to realize your dream?

- *Structure.* How do you want to be structured? Will you have a board? Do you anticipate having employees? Are there others who will be involved in the operations or oversight? Do you want to become a 501 (c)(3) nonprofit or a for-profit organization? If for-profit, what kind of designation? (It might be important for you to seek out a lawyer for legal advice, as we did.)

  Question. What kind of organizational structure do you envision will best suit your dream?

- *Services.* What services do you want to provide? What do you want to offer to meet the needs of the world's or your community's deep hunger? As we have worked through our services, we have focused on three: offering spiritual direction and training and support for spiritual directors, providing space for and supporting individuals who want to get away for a personal retreat, and providing sacred space for small groups and teams to get away for retreats or to do important work.

Question. What services do you hope to provide through realizing your dream? What kinds of work do you "most need to do" and are qualified to offer?

Take your time to reflect on each section and write down your answers in your journal. Record what you know to date. As time goes on, you can add to it. Remember that none of these answers are set in stone. You can and likely will change some of them as your dream comes more clearly into focus.

INTERVIEW

Dave Baldwin and Furnace Hills Coffee

*I*N 2010 DAVE BALDWIN SAID HE "kind of backed into his dream through a family crisis." Dave had been a pastor for most of his adult life and had recently moved from the Midwest to Furnace Hills, Maryland, to become an executive pastor in a local church. In addition, he and his wife, Louise, had an adult daughter, Erin, with Down syndrome, who had been living in a residential center in the Midwest, but it became apparent that she needed to move back home with them.

Dave was concerned for Erin. He wanted her to feel purposeful and have a meaningful life and work. In a serendipitous moment on Facebook, he read about an organization that was starting a coffee roasting company and employing adults with developmental disabilities. That idea inspired him and set into motion his own process of learning about and exploring the coffee roasting business. The real test came when he taught Erin how to roast coffee beans and discovered that she not only could, but indeed, loved to roast them!

Dave explained,

We had a home roaster in the house—the kind you had to watch to know when they were done. Erin started roasting beans and was a natural. Before long, we had coffee beans in the kitchen, dining room and lower level of house. Finally, we moved to a storefront in Westminster and hired someone to help. One thing led to another.

In 2010 Dave founded Furnace Hills Coffee, a gourmet specialty coffee business that supplies customers with freshly roasted bags of specialty coffee, delivered right to their doorsteps. But beyond roasting great coffee, Dave had another mission in mind. He was moved by the fact that 78 percent of adults with developmental disabilities are under-employed or unemployed. That statistic troubled him. So, when he started Furnace Hills, he determined that the mission would be to employ Erin and other adults with developmental disabilities—*special coffee roasted by special people.*

Not only was Dave guided by his passion to roast great coffee and his mission to employ adults with disabilities, he also had his own set of values that began to shape his business practices. He began to care about social responsibility and traceability. As a result, Furnace Hills green coffee beans are only sourced from specialty coffee merchants who have intimate, long-term working relationships with coffee farms and cooperatives. "We love the fact that our coffees are totally traceable. In fact, not only can we tell you the name of the farmer who grew the coffee beans, but we can probably tell you the name of his wife and kids too."

Though Dave didn't have a background in business, he has worked hard developing his dream and has sought out people to speak into his life who know the world of business. Early on he also discovered important resources—books, websites and podcasts—that have helped mature him and his business savvy. Through his commitment to educating himself and developing good business practices, loyal customers who buy Furnace Hills coffee beans know they can count on the highest environmental, business and roasting standards possible.

Our roasting philosophy is centered on the simple principle that the spectacular coffees cultivated by our partners at origin deserve the utmost respect while under our care. Driven by a passionate pursuit of coffee perfection, we lovingly sight roast each coffee in a separate, small batch to bring out each bean's magnificent flavors and aromas.

Some might call Dave a coffee snob, and he probably wouldn't mind. But behind his sophisticated taste buds is a man with a dream to provide his customers with the very best-tasting cup of coffee possible through the fairest means and roasted by special people with abilities that are often overlooked.

7

SORTING

There are all different kinds of voices calling you to all different kinds of work, and the problem is to find out which is the voice of God rather than of Society, say, or the Super-ego, or Self-interest. By and large a good rule for finding out is this: The kind of work God usually calls you to is the kind of work (a) that you most need to do and (b) that the world most needs to have done.

Frederick Buechner

MY HUSBAND AND I HAVE DIFFERENT ideas about what constitutes trash and what constitutes treasure. He's a collector; I'm a purger. He feels most at home surrounded by a prolific and random collection of rocks, fishing reels, painted glass, old guitars, and numerous art pieces and photographs. I'm a minimalist. I'm most at home within a visually pleasing ambiance that is sparse and uncluttered. But for both of us, when it has come to sorting through the vast array of creative ideas we've had about our dream, it's been difficult at times to know what to throw away and what to keep.

It's like when you're going through your clothes closet and creating piles of what to save and what to give to Goodwill. It's a tedious and sometimes agonizing process to decide whether to give away that prized sweatshirt from college or those trendy but in-perfect-shape pants from a couple of seasons ago. During the creative process of giving birth to a dream, you will need to sort through the abundant collection of ideas and musings you've had related to your new venture. In fact, throughout the life of your dream, you will need to become adept at recognizing what goes with it and what doesn't.

That's why it's important to learn to befriend the following questions: What belongs and what doesn't? What do I keep and what do I give away? What opportunities do I say yes to and what opportunities do I say no to? Buechner's quote defines our dilemma well: "There are all different kinds of voices calling you to all different kinds of work, and the problem is to find out which is the voice of God."

DEVELOPING CRITERIA

So, how do we sort through the pile of ideas we've gathered during our planning stage and decide which ones fit our dream and which ones need to go? For some of you right now I can almost feel your panic. Like my dear husband, the thought of letting go of something creates immense anxiety and heart palpitations. What if you'll need it someday? What if you forget about it and it's just the thing that you might be looking for at another time. Relax. The great thing about sorting through your wardrobe of ideas is that the closet size isn't an issue! You can keep them tucked away in a file on your computer or in a notebook where they will be safe if and when you need to find them in the future.

So, think about how you do it when you go through the clothes in your closet. I usually think about whether that particular sweater or skirt fits, whether I like it, if I've worn it recently, and if I have occasions to wear it. For instance, I have a fur coat from my husband's grandmother that is stuffed way in the back of my closet. I haven't had the nerve to get rid of it, and yet there is zero chance I will ever wear it. Should I keep it?

The answer to that question lies in the criteria I use to determine what stays in my closet and what goes. In the same way, when we have a dream in the making, we will need to develop some prayerful criteria to evaluate the ideas, opportunities, programs, initiatives or next steps we take related to our vision. There are three questions you can ponder in prayer when you begin to sort through with God what belongs to your dream and what doesn't:

- Does it fit the dream God's given me?
- Is it the right time?
- Is there another reason beyond reason to say yes?

DOES IT FIT THE DREAM GOD'S GIVEN ME?

Most creative processes are messy and by nature generate a vast assortment of inspirations and imaginings. As God makes clear the vision, mission, values and scope of your dream, you will be more capable of discerning what to say yes to and what to say no to. That sounds easier than it sometimes is. It's often trial by error or testing it out. In the theoretical stages of planning, you might have an idea that seems God-inspired, but when it's time to try it, it doesn't fit as well as you thought it would. So, you have to become proficient at asking the question "God, does this fit the vision you've given me?"

- Does it fit the vision and mission of this dream as I understand it?
- Would saying yes to this support and reflect the values God has instilled in me?
- Does it fit the scope of my dream (who it serves) and my God-given capacity? Is it beyond me or an invitation to trust God and stretch myself?

One of the realities we've faced as we've lived into our dream is that because David and I both have other work we do (he's a career counselor and I'm a spiritual director and congregational consultant), one of our limiting factors is our own capacity. We've had more requests than we can say yes to without burning ourselves out. We've had to say no or not yet to some energizing and creative ideas that we'd love to do, simply because we don't have the bandwidth for them right now.

Does it fit? is an important criteria to use to sort through and determine what belongs and what goes into a discard pile or file for later use.

IS IT THE RIGHT TIME?

As you consider potential elements of your dream, another important evaluation criterion is whether it's the right time. Though something might seem right in terms of fit—it fits the mission, aligns with the vision and is within the scope—you also need to be able to imagine it. When you live it out in your mind, try it on for size, does it seem like the right time?

There are situations when an idea seems like it should fit, but something holds you back from saying yes to it. You might not be able to explain why or justify to others your reasons for adding it to the "on hold" or "question mark" pile, but you have to put it there any way. It's either not time or the answer isn't clear. But if you can't imagine doing it without a serious check in your spirit or heart burn, then consider putting it on the shelf for a while. The Spirit is speaking to you.

Many of the people I interviewed had to give up initially on an aspect of their dream, even though that idea sounded good, until a later and better time in the gestation of their dream. Take for instance Abby Kuzma as she started the Neighborhood Christian Legal Clinic. She and her volunteers knew there was a need for pro bono legal assistance among local immigrants, but initially it was not well-received. They discovered that these immigrants didn't trust them. It took time to build trust and establish relationships before immigrants would come to the clinic for help.

IS THERE ANOTHER REASON BEYOND REASON?

Even if an idea has failed the test for fit or timeliness, there's still cause, at times, to make an exception. Like the fur coat in my closet, I hang on to it and don't give it away because of the person it belonged to who gave it to me. I feel nostalgic about it. When I think of David's grandma, I smile, remembering who she was, how she lived a humble life and loved beautiful things. Though I'll likely never wear it, there's a reason beyond reason to keep it.

In the same way, you will have your own criteria that God instills in you over time that won't always make sense. It's your prerogative to decide if something belongs, if you want to say yes, just because—because it's something you believe God is in, because it's for someone you care deeply about, because you made a promise.

We offer our first floor for small groups and teams to come and do sacred work. We want to support people and organizations that we believe are doing God's kingdom work, whether they are traditional ministries or not. One of those groups is the Oaks Academy—our first guests and our neighbors. This wonderful classical Christian school is just down the street from us. We love the influence they're having in our neighborhood; we love their philosophy of education; we love the faculty and staff. And because of that, we host them. And my guess is we will always host them because of our loyalty to them. No, they don't necessarily fall in line with our purpose to teach and model contemplative practices that help individuals discover their calling and live a sustainable life of faith, but they do fall in line with our instincts to be a good neighbor.

So, as you begin to make sense of the mound of creative expressions of how to live out your dream, pay attention to the criteria that God is instilling in you to help you evaluate what to keep, what to store and what to let go of. These tools will undoubtedly help you say yes to what is important and viable as you live your God-given dream with integrity.

TAKING HALF-STEPS

One of the ways our friend, Dave Baldwin, has learned to distinguish what belongs with his dream and what doesn't is through measuring each new direction or next step by "half-steps." When Dave started Furnace Hills Coffee, one of the first commitments he made was that they would "major in half-steps."

Half-steps are modest, reasonable steps forward that are measured by their company's capacity. They ask the question, "What can we do without risking our mission and the health of our company and employees?" Half-steps are progress, just slower progress. If an opportunity comes along that is too large a leap, then Dave knows it's not for them. Half-steps fit the company culture and have become a litmus test for how Dave identifies what aligns with the approach of Furnace Hills Coffee and what doesn't.

Dave shared,

How do you know the difference between a half-step and beyond? It's based on capacity. For instance, we use a modest $3,500 roaster. We could buy a $40,000 roaster, but that would be beyond our capacity. We add as we go rather than have production catch up with expansion.

Dave shared a current example of how this criterion of measurement helped him sort out an opportunity that came his way.

We're in the process right now of evaluating an opportunity. The guy who owns the building [where the roasting company is located] wants to sell it to us and give me $100,000 to invest in our business. It feels like too big a step. It would take us off-track. We'd have to find tenants and keep up with a building. That doesn't feel like a half-step.

Dave recognized in this opportunity the danger of getting off course from the mission of Furnace Hills, from roasting coffee beans to becoming a landlord and building supervisor. For some who would receive an offer like this it might appear to be too good to refuse. But for Dave, he recognized it as too far a reach. That's how he and Erin and Furnace Hills Coffee roll—one half-step at a time. (Oh, and by the way, if you visit us at Sustainable Faith Indy, you will be offered an unforgettable cup of java made from organic, fair trade coffee beans, which were roasted by the special people at Furnace Hills Coffee!)

REFLECTION: LEARNING TO SORT THINGS OUT

Learning to sort through your prolific collection of ideas will require you to develop some specific criteria for evaluating them. I've suggested questions related to fit, timing and intuition—a reason beyond reason. What I recommend, in addition to these categories, is for you to take some time to jot down any other God-given gauges for evaluation. Perhaps you've become convinced that your dream should never impinge on your personal savings or your commitment to being home five nights a week. You know what has become important to you, what you don't want to risk, in the midst of taking the risk of birthing a God-given dream.

It might be helpful to practice sorting by thinking about a couple of things you're considering doing related to your dream right now. Use them as practice; take each one through the sorting process and see what conclusions you come to.

1. Begin by stating the opportunity you are considering.

2. Does it fit your understanding of the vision and mission of your dream? Explain.

3. Does it seem like the right time? If so, why? If not, why not?

4. Is there a reason beyond reason why you should say yes to this idea or opportunity? Explain.

5. Finally, take some time and write down any other criteria, convictions or commitments that need to inform the decisions you make and opportunities you take on. Use those to evaluate the ideas you are sorting through.

INTERVIEW

Joanna Taft and the Harrison Center for the Arts

*I*F YOU LIVED IN THE CITY OF INDIANAPOLIS and did much hobnobbing it wouldn't take long before you'd hear the names Bill and Joanna Taft. They've been deeply involved for more than twenty years in what they believe to be their calling as a family—the healing of the city. And they don't understand that call to simply be one of prayer but of action, sacrifice and grassroots involvement. From an urban neighborhood park to an inner city church to an urban classical grade school and high school, the Tafts have put their hands and hearts to work to bring both spiritual and tangible revitalization to the city they love.

After a number of years being involved in government work, Joanna begins her story:

> I saw my heart moving toward community development. I worked for Indiana Landmarks [an organization that saves and protects historic places]. It was my entry into community development. I began to understand the importance of community and what it looked like to be a healthy neighborhood. Bill and I started to understand how healing a neighborhood wasn't just bricks and mortar; there were other pieces as well, like educating homeowners, starting libraries, establishing businesses and third places where people come together.

Soon after, the Tafts bought a boarded up house and moved into an urban neighborhood. Joanna remembers being afraid, and then she started to meet other neighbors living inside their homes who were scared as well. She and her neighbors began to dream together about a neighborhood park and worked on getting one established. Not long after, Joanna became acquainted with a group of gifted women who wanted to plant a Christian elementary school in the inner city. Joanna got involved and eventually joined the board of the Oaks Academy, and the Tafts were one of the founding families—their kids were in the first class. For five years, Joanna worked as a volunteer developing the infrastructure.

About the same time the Tafts were going to a church in the suburbs and felt a big disconnect between working and playing downtown and then leaving on Sunday to worship. One day, Joanna's former boss from Landmark called and said that there was a historic church building close to their home that needed an owner. "You should start a church." "Bill and I thought about it. We're not pastors!" they protested.

But because the Tafts are curious people with an eye for the Spirit's work and energy to boot, they took this as a sign that God might be nudging them and considered the next logical step: they called a pastor they knew who was good at church planting. They told him that they were interested in possibly planting a downtown church. He challenged them to pray daily and promised to do the same. A month later, he called and asked if Bill and Joanna wanted to go on a vision trip to visit some urban churches in New York City. They did—and one of the churches was Redeemer Presbyterian. Their hearts were ignited, and soon after, the Tafts, along with a handful of other interested families, initiated the planting of Redeemer Presbyterian Church in Indianapolis.

The church began to meet in the historic building and eventually was able to purchase it from the owner, who was a local arts philanthropist. His vision had been to develop the space into an art center and gallery, but because of the many repairs and expense maintaining it, it became a financial drain.

Once Redeemer purchased the building from him, a group of leaders began a conversation about what to do with the extra, unused space. Joanna suggested what the previous owner had in mind—an art center—and was given charge to develop a plan and start what is now called the Harrison Center for the Arts. The Harrison Center houses four galleries and twenty-four studios currently shared by thirty-six artists. Each first Friday of the month it opens its doors to hundreds of folks who Joanna Taft hopes will become patrons of the arts and world-class citizens through exposure to culture and contemporary art.

As Joanna mused about what she's learned realizing her dream to be a city healer, she believes, "If you're passionate enough and you don't give up, you will be successful. Now when people ask me to do things, even if it's scary, I say yes. I lean into the fear. The more I do that, the more I see community built."

8

CHANGING

Indeed, the notion that it is wrong for one to change his mind is antithetical to the most basic principle of education—that we can grow and make progress through the accumulation of knowledge. If we want to accomplish anything substantive, both as a nation and as individuals, we need to embrace inconsistency when it is called for, support contradiction when it makes sense, and celebrate flip-flopping when it results in a positive change. This I believe.

Michael, a high school student

*A*S I MENTIONED EARLIER, one of the most formidable challenges I faced early on was how I would give birth to this dream of founding an urban retreat center with my husband's support but not his involvement. In the beginning, whenever we discussed it, David would remind me that he's an introvert and the idea of living in a space where we had a constant flow of people in and out just didn't fit him. I would sigh, try not to pout and say to him, "I understand." And so I began to plan for this dream accordingly.

Then something unexpected happened. David and I spent time that summer at a gorgeous home and retreat center near Lexington, Virginia,

called the Bellfry. The dwelling is situated on a picturesque knoll, surrounded by the Blue Ridge Mountains. Each morning, coffee and blanket
in hand, we would make a short trek to a grassy crest and watch the
sunrise. It was like welcoming the face of God as the sun peeped over the
ridge and warm rays of light spilled through the twilight.

During our time, we experienced not only the beauty of this restor-
ative setting, but we observed our host, Anne Grizzle, one of the founders
and visionaries of the Bellfry. When we arrived, her first act of kindness
was to stoop and wash our feet. Anne seemed capable of not only hosting
us but also listening deeply to our hearts as she offered the gift of presence.
When I shared my dream with her, she responded enthusiastically. "Go
for it! After all, you're in the prime of your life!" Wow. No one had said
that to me in a long time!

While there, subtly and unsuspectingly, David became curious and
more open about what it might be like for us to offer hospitality in a
retreat setting. He didn't say anything to me until after we left the Bellfry
and spent another week of vacation in Asheville, North Carolina.
Throughout the following days, we processed our experience and talked
deeply about the implications of what it might mean for us—only with
one curve ball—the setting. David couldn't envision himself in an urban
location, but he could in a rural one.

As I observed his heart warming toward this dream, and we contem-
plated our mutual love for nature and its repairing qualities, I had to
wrestle with letting go of my initial vision of a retreat center in the city.
There were some losses involved, like nearness to our family and proximity to those we would host. In addition, to consider a change of location and vision felt risky, like I was a flip-flopper—someone who didn't
really know what she wanted. And I wondered how others with whom I
had shared my original vision would react. Would they question the
clarity of my vision and the strength of my commitment?

IT'S OKAY TO CHANGE MY MIND

During this time, I wrote in a blog post:

As I reflect on this last year, I notice a pattern emerge that makes me sort of uncomfortable. It looks an awful lot like flip-flopping. I have changed my mind, gone back and forth, discovered and re-discovered what I believe to be God's path forward for me as it relates to starting Sustainable Faith Indy. Yet, as I reflect on how God is speaking to me through this year in retrospect, I see that this circuitous path is helping me discover God's will. I'm learning that *it's okay to change my mind.*

Because you know the end of our story, you also know that we eventually returned to the vision of an urban retreat center. So, we flip-flopped again! But this time, we did so together. Perhaps the visit to the Bellfry was the experience David needed to overcome inertia, to awaken to God's dream for him and us. From there we were able to discern our path together. And this wasn't the only change we've made throughout the birthing process. We've changed direction in other ways and are *still* making adjustments, even as we live our dream. What we have now come to expect and accept is that *it's okay to change our minds.*

I agree with Michael, the articulate high school student I quoted at the beginning of the chapter. There can be virtue in flip-flopping. Changing our minds is part of the educational process, the natural by-product of accumulating knowledge along the journey of life.

However, being open to change is a tricky thing. Let me explain what I mean by making a comparison to sailing a boat. If we were the captain of a ship, we would want to make sure that our sails were open and responsive to the wind *and* our rudder stalwart toward our destination. If we wanted to sail from the Florida Keys to the Bahamas, there are many routes we could take, but we'd better make sure we are heading south or we might end up in Boston. So, as we are involved in the creative work of realizing a dream, we will need to change some of our ideas; we may zigzag back and forth, again and again. Concurrently, we need to remain true to the mission of our dream. I observed this very dynamic at work during my interview with Joanna Taft.

THE HEALING OF THE CITY

Learning to be responsive to the winds of the Spirit, Joanna and Bill Taft's approach to living their dream is probably the most dynamic illustration of what I described in the introduction as "way leads to way." They began with a heart to see their city healed. They got involved in the things they were learning about healing a city. And one zig led to the next zag; one neighborhood park, two schools, a church and a center for the arts later, the Tafts continue to invest in opportunities that have potential to make Indianapolis a more vibrant, world-class city.

When the conversation began with leaders from Redeemer Presbyterian Church about how to use the unused space in their building, Joanna was aware that the previous owner had intended to turn it into an art gallery and studios. So, she asked the pivotal question "Why can't a church love a neighborhood through opening an art gallery?" She has learned to do that, to ask the questions that others might not consider or even think to be off course. Do churches open art galleries? Really? She has learned to ask questions with a slant, questions that lead to strategic change.

As Joanna looked back on that experience, she ruminated,

> I didn't have a background in contemporary art. I knew one artist—Kyle Ragsdale. Yet, the church hired me to develop the Harrison Center. I kept thinking to myself, *What matters is faith expressed in love.*
>
> I remember Kyle and I walked through the building and decided we'd charge $100 a month for each studio. After a year and a half, so many people were flooding the First Friday events that we realized we needed to start a not-for-profit.

First Friday is now a big happening all over Indianapolis and surrounding suburbs as galleries and churches—and even funeral homes—open their doors to the public, free of charge, sharing art collections and celebrating culture—the healing of a city! The Harrison Center for the Arts is one of those healing projects, and Joanna is one of those people

who has learned to embrace opportunity and change, but hold on tight
to the mission.

DISCOVERING PROVIDENCE *Blog on This Theme*

Sometimes, in fact, the invitations to adjust our course are what lead to
providential opportunities. Providence may sound like an old-fashioned
word, but it's a great word with a wonderful meaning. It describes the
invisible hand of God guiding us through the circumstances of our lives.
It's the underlying principle of "way leads to way," a description of how
God guides us by divinely connecting what can appear to be the disparate
dots of our lives.

God's providence doesn't imply that everything that happens in our
lives is from God, but that God can direct us through what happens. I
think one of the signs of spiritual maturity is an increased sensitivity to
God's guidance and noticing providential opportunities. The apostle Paul
is a great example of someone who was adept at discovering providence.

Paul, a writer of much of the New Testament, was a well-traveled soul.
He zigzagged all over the known world as an ambassador for Christ. He
also learned how to pay attention to when the Holy Spirit was leading
him to take an alternate route, one that he hadn't planned to take. He
would be one place and then attempt to go to another, but would change
his mind, discerning that the Spirit was preventing him.

In one example Paul and his companions came to the border of an
ancient region called Mysia and tried to enter another region, "but the
Spirit of Jesus would not allow them to. So they passed by Mysia and
went down to Troas" (Acts 16:7-8 NIV). What happened shortly after was
a departure to Philippi and a serendipitous meeting with a group of
women, one of whom was Lydia, a wealthy merchant. Lydia became a
follower of Jesus, was baptized, opened her home to Paul and his companions, and established a house church.

We don't know what means the Spirit of Jesus used to direct Paul in
his coming and going. In one instance, he had a dream as he was sleeping
and was told where to go next. It could have been that he learned to

discern a spiritual hunch through praying. Or maybe he and his companions attempted to go to a place and natural circumstances, like the region's governing rulers, wouldn't permit them. Whatever the means of direction, it appeared that Paul—a pretty headstrong person at times— was okay with being rerouted, changing directions and changing his mind about where he was headed next. In this case, the delightful result was a God-ordained encounter.

REFLECTION: STANDING AT THE CROSSROADS

One question you will face as you embark on the voyage toward realizing your dream is what changes or adjustments to make along the way. In each moment, at each crossroads, you will need to discern which are being initiated by the Spirit of Jesus and which could land you in Boston. How will you be responsive to change without losing your way?

You will undoubtedly come to intersections where you see roads to the right and left, roads behind you and before you, and you will have to decide which way is forward. If or when you find yourself at a place like this, here is a spiritual direction process that might help you discern the providence of God for you.

- Read the following verse, slowly and contemplatively, several times.

> This is what the LORD says:
>   "Stand at the crossroads and look;
>   ask for the ancient paths,
> ask where the good way is, and walk in it,
>   and you will find rest for your souls." (Jeremiah 6:16 NIV)

- What stands out to you? How does this verse resonate with you right now?

- If you are at an intersection or crossroads, aware of two or more directions you could go, describe each of your options.

- Make a list of all the virtues (the good way) of each option.

- Make a list of any negative features of each option.

- Which option, if you were to take it, would lead to rest? Or, another way to put it, which option resonates most peacefully with your mind, heart and spirit?

- What does it mean to you and your dream to ask God "for the ancient path"? What intuitions do you have about that?

- What is your next step in taking that path?

As you amble along this path with twists and turns and intersections, you will come to many crossroads where you must pause and ask where to go. Ask for the ancient path. Look for the good way. And once you commit to a route, remember that if a ways down the road something about it doesn't seem right—*it's okay to change your mind.*

INTERVIEW

Nate Hershey and City Life Wheels

NATE HERSHEY HAS ALWAYS BEEN ambidextrous in terms of his interests. On the one hand he loves poetry, nature and all things Wendell Berry. On the other he loves tinkering with mechanical things, wood working and doing hands-on projects around the house. Yet beyond his divergent proclivities, Nate has always had a tender heart for young people.

In Nate's words,

A lot of what I care about comes from a deeper place of wanting to support kids—kids who are really myself—kids who want to be delighted in. I think there's a small place in me that has always wanted to experience the delight of God, a tender, insecure spot. I personally identify with the underdog on an emotional level. I often feel shy and uncertain. So, I've always been drawn to kids, found it easy to enter into their worlds and empathize. When I see someone who struggles to believe that they are valuable, loved—that they have something to offer the world—my heart just breaks for that person.

Nate began to "dream" his dream while he was working for an organization mentoring at-risk youth. He described a moment when something clicked for him:

I'm in the living room with Edward; he's six. The only things you can get him to be excited about are video games. But what really struck me was his single mom, who had five other kids and no space to delight in Edward. She didn't know how to connect with him emotionally. I saw this in many—most—kids at that school. They didn't know the deeper things, to love and be loved, to connect relationally with others. I wondered to myself, *How is this kid going to survive?*

Time after time, I saw so many like Edward—kids who needed to know that the Father loved them and that they had something to offer the world. And I realized that for them to experience this, it had to be tangible. It needed to be tactile in nature.

The more Nate thought about this, the more convinced he became that the best way into their worlds and hearts was through some kind of practical, tangible service. Something he could offer them, train them in that would help them experience "the Father's love" and, in turn, help them feel like they had something valuable to offer.

Eventually, I had the idea that training youth in automotive repair could be a way, because so many of these kid's moms—single moms—needed cars to get around. But I didn't know how to work on cars. Up to that point I'd done one brake job and an oil change. I was mechanically oriented—a Lego kid—but never into cars. So, basically, I would be starting from scratch.

Soon after, Nate enrolled in an automotive repair program at a local trade school. He spent $20,000 toward a degree. After he finished his training, he described how humbling it was to have a bachelor's degree and begin working at a repair shop while making bottom-level pay, changing oil, no less. Car repair is dirty work. In the winter, you freeze to death; in the summer you sweat to death. And Nate sweat it out—for a very long time.

Though Nate Hershey waited eight long, humbling years for his vision to be realized, one day he heard about a new initiative of Youth for Christ (YFC) in Indianapolis called City Life Wheels—a mentoring program for at-risk youth, training them in how to maintain and repair cars. YFC's vision also included giving youth an opportunity to work on their families' cars and introducing the kids and their families to Christ in the process. Youth for Christ was looking for a director—and Nate, quite obviously, fit the bill! Nate and his staff and volunteers have recently opened the doors of City Life Wheels in a garage on the Near Eastside and are doing the very thing he dreamed of doing.

It's hard work and Nate has often felt the weight and questioned whether he has what it takes. Yet he's also discovering that the youth he mentors and trains aren't the only ones impacted by this dream. So is he.

Nate shared,

Being a son, an heir of the Father (Galatians 4:6), has started to personally sink into me. Because of the heaviness of this vision, I want to live into the very thing I coach these youth toward—that God delights in me as his son. If I'm going to convey to these youth that God delights in them, I'd better believe it myself.

9

WAITING

*I work very hard every afternoon from 4:30 to 4:40—that being the limit
of the light I represent. You must not paint everything you see.
You must wait, and wait patiently, until the exceptional,
the wonderful effect or aspect comes.*

Winslow Homer

*T*HE ABOVE WORDS WERE INSCRIBED on a large wall at the Art
Institute of Chicago during a special exhibit of Winslow Homer's
paintings. I saw it after I had stood before a number of his paintings,
absolutely in awe of the light he so determinedly sought to represent.
Homer's paintings are often dark and shadowy with a wash of light so
translucent and real that it's as though a physical light was shining on
the subject. I found myself pondering these words for days after I visited
this exhibit and wondered if there was anything in life that I was *that*
patient to wait for.

Truth be told, I'm a bad waiter. If a score were given to waiting—10
being the highest and 1 being the lowest—I'm pretty sure I would get at
best a 2. I'm a getter-doner. I don't like to wait. Don't see the need to wait.
Think waiting is a waste of time. And so when God, whom I believe
would score a 10 on the waiting scale, has asked me to wait, I've not responded with tremendous gratitude or joy.

Yet, when it comes to the business of birthing a dream, waiting is inevitably a part of the process. I don't know anyone who has attempted to start a new venture that hasn't encountered delays. Those delays can sometimes cause the dreamer to question whether God is really behind and in support of the dream or resolutely opposed to it.

SWEATING IT OUT

Of all the people I know who've had to wait patiently for the door to open to their dream—I don't know anyone who has done so with more grace and resolve then our friend Nate Hershey. For eight years Nate waited as he worked in two different garages learning the car repair trade while simultaneously trying to develop and keep his dream alive. As time went on, he began to envision more clearly and desire more intensely what it was he wanted to do.

Nate described what it was like:

At first the waiting was comfortable—easy, because I knew the dream I had would take a lot of work, and I needed some time just to get to know the automotive industry. So there was little pressure to make it all happen right away. As I moved on to a different repair shop for additional experience, I enjoyed more challenging work, but restlessness emerged more and more. I loved working with my hands, but I wanted my work to make a difference in the lives of people—to invoke change and the development of a person, and I wanted to see this dream take place.

Nate said that the hardest part was sticking with it and to keep believing that what he was doing was worthwhile.

I also struggled with motivation to kick-start it, often feeling as if I didn't have the gifts to make it all happen. That was the truth. I needed a team; I needed others who could dream with me, who could play roles that seemed daunting to me. I often felt a silence from God. As I struggled with doubt about my ability to pull it together, I wondered how God was a part of it at all, if he was leading me at all.

THE CRUCIBLE OF WAITING

As David and I spent elongated time waiting for our house to sell—the first step toward realizing our dream—we began to wonder whether God was obstructing the way forward. Our house had a "For Sale" sign in the yard for eight months. We showed it seventy-two times. We had three rollercoaster offers that were bogus or fell through. Every time I got a text from the showing service, we'd kick it into high gear, scurry around thinking, *This could be the one!* and relocate for two hours or more with our dog and sometimes daughter in tow. (Did I mention that David and I both work from home?) It was like responding to seventy-two unexpected fire drills—equally nerve-racking and exhausting.

Not only were we drained by the ordeal of trying to sell our house, we were also disappointed from trying to buy one. We knew we were looking for a unique property, and there were very few that fit our criteria in our price range. Three times we watched properties that we had "fallen in love with" sell, while we waited for our house to sell. As each one slipped through our fingers, we became increasingly confused. All of this caused deep consternation as we battled whether to continue or just throw in the towel.

I tried to be patient. I tried to have the posture of Winslow Homer and wait, hoping the perfect light would dawn and God's path forward would appear. But I scored a 2 in my efforts. No, truthfully, more like a -2.

In *Falling Upward: Spirituality for the Two Halves of Life*, Richard Rohr describes the very spot I found myself in. He writes,

Sooner or later, if you are on any classic "spiritual schedule," some event, person, death, idea or relationship will enter your life that you simply cannot deal with, using your present skill set, your acquired knowledge, or your strong willpower. Spiritually speaking, you will be, you must be, led to the edge of your own private resources. At that point you will stumble over a necessary stumbling stone, as Isaiah calls it; or to state it in our language here, you will and you must "lose" at something. This is the only way that Life-Fate-God-Grace-Mystery can get you to change, let go of your egocentric preoccupations, and go the further and larger journey.

Take a minute to digest those words. They might be worth re-reading.

Have you ever been led to the edge of your own private resources? Have you stumbled over a necessary stumbling stone? Lost at something you desired deeply? If you are gestating a God-given dream, it might be, though not a given, that you will find yourself in the place that Rohr describes.

We came to that edge. We were ready to give up. We had no more resources to spend on this wacky dream. And frankly, what I saw coming out of me was disturbing. I saw a willfulness emerge with bulldozer force and determination to see this dream through. But there was nothing I could do to make it happen. I struggled to comprehend how to hold such full and strong desire in my heart for something I believed to be God's desire for me without a place to channel it. I didn't know how to both wait *and* persevere—something that seemed necessary if I was going to give this dream a go.

THE MOTHER OF ALL WAITING-ON-GOD STORIES

So, to get some perspective on this waiting game, take a moment with me to consider the mother of all waiting-on-God stories in the Bible: the story of Abraham who received a God-prompted dream that took twenty-five years to begin to fulfill! God came to him at the age of seventy-five and asked Abraham (Abram) to leave his native land and travel with his wife, Sarah (Sarai), to a land that God would show them (Genesis 12:1). He promised Abraham, who was fatherless at the time, that he would make him the father of many. Not just many children, many nations. And *twenty-five years later*, Abraham and Sarah gave birth to their first son, Isaac.

During the wait, Abraham, out of his own willfulness, tried to help God out. If Sarah, his wife, wasn't going to conceive, then he and Sarah decided that maybe her maid, Hagar, would do. And so Abraham slept with Hagar and she bore a son, Ishmael (Genesis 16). Waiting got the best of them. And for many who carry a heart full of desire and imagination for what they believe to be a God-given dream, waiting can be the straw that breaks the camel's back.

BENEATH THE WAITING

This is one of the more painful stories in the Bible for me to read. I really hate how long it took for God to fulfill the vision that he gave to Abraham. But I want to take a pause from this story and then return to it, as we consider what might be beneath the waiting in his story, as well as our own.

Waiting doesn't always bring out the best in us, does it? But it can be the impetus to learn a deeper form of trust in and surrender to God. Someone by the name of Ignatius of Loyola called this posture "holy indifference." Holy or active indifference isn't what it sounds like. *Indifference* is a word that typically has negative connotations. It suggests apathy, an unfeeling disconnect toward someone or something that I should care about. For many who hold a dream in our hearts, it's the antithesis of how we feel about it. We care deeply. We're rarely indifferent.

But in the way that Ignatius meant it, holy or active indifference is the attitude of doing what we can to pursue God's will, but entrusting the outcome to God. We embrace the deep and true desires of our heart, but remain "detached" from their ultimate fulfillment. We place what we desire and believe to be the will of God "on the altar." Now back to Abraham's story.

Though much happened to Sarah and Abraham over the course of the twenty-five years they waited for God's fulfillment of this dream—and I'm sure they weren't just sitting around *only* waiting—God was doing a deep work in Abraham's heart: a work of transforming his willfulness into willingness, his grasping into letting go, his manipulation into trusting surrender.

Never did Abraham's character and trust in God shine more brightly than when he responded with holy indifference to God's request that he sacrifice his son Isaac on an altar (Genesis 22:1-18). I offer this part of the story gently, for as much as it is a foreshadowing of God sacrificing his Son, it's still a disturbing request for God to make of a father. To Abraham maybe it wasn't as outrageous a notion as it is to us, given that in his ancient culture child sacrifice to "the gods" was not uncommon. And it seems clear from his response to Isaac that Abraham trusted in God to intervene *somehow*. Just the same, it's part of the story that's really hard to know what to do with.

When Abraham and Isaac made their way to the spot where God told Abraham to go and sacrifice his son, Isaac turned to his dad and asked where the sheep for the burnt offering was. "God will provide," Abraham replied, with a peculiar confidence. Then Abraham tied Isaac to an altar he had built and picked up the knife to kill his son. Suddenly, a voice from heaven, the angel of the Lord, called out, "Abraham! Abraham!"

"Yes," Abraham replied. "Here I am!" . . .

"This is what the LORD says: Because you have obeyed me and have not withheld even your son, your only son, I swear by my own name that I will certainly bless you. I will multiply your descendants beyond number, like the stars in the sky and the sand on the seashore. Your descendants will conquer the cities of their enemies. And through your descendants all the nations of the earth will be blessed—all because you have obeyed me." (Genesis 22:11, 16-18)

And just as Abraham so confidently anticipated, God did provide a ram, caught in a nearby briar, for the sacrifice.

Through twenty-five years of waiting on God, and on more than one occasion willfully taking matters into his own hands, this scene vividly depicts what Ignatius was describing with the term holy indifference. Abraham had learned to hold God's dream with an open hand, to surrender this dream to God, to entrust his dream to God as his dream keeper.

REFLECTION: IN THE WAITING ROOM

If you find yourself having protracted times of waiting to birth your dream, one of the values this experience provides is the chance to confront your own willfulness. Waiting serves a very important purpose because it teaches us to "let go," "to come to the edge, to an end of our resources." It's one means through which God loosens the grip of our ego and changes us.

If or when you find yourself in the waiting room, the following are some questions to reflect on that might help you gain some perspective and discern the nature of your energy as you expend yourself toward your dream. I've found Margaret Silf's book on Ignatian spirituality, called *The Inner Compass*, a helpful guide in sensitizing me to the quality and source of my inner drives. Silf explains, "The action of God on our lives is always, at its heart, experienced as a drawing. If we are feeling driven, then the prompting that gives rise to it is not from God but from the force fields of our own (or other people's) kingdoms."

1. How would you describe the energy, the "action of God," that you have toward your dream? Drawn or driven? Willing or willful? At times both?

2. If you notice driven or willful energy, when do you most experience it? What is going on? *Perpetuated by fear, uncertainty*

3. Winslow Homer said, "You must wait, and wait patiently, until the exceptional, the wonderful effect or aspect comes." If you are in a season of waiting, what do you think is going on? Is there any exceptional, wonderful effect that you sense God is up to?

4. In order to develop an attitude of holy indifference, you will need to surrender the outcome of your dream to God. What would that feel like to do so right now?

5. If you are ready, take some time in prayer to offer your dream to God. Consider creating a small visual representation of an altar that symbolizes your surrender, a rock or small pile of rocks, a piece of

driftwood, a special candle or something similar. Place it in a spot where you will see it each day and be reminded of your surrendering your dream to God.

INTERVIEW

Melissa Millis and Nou Hope

*N*OU HOPE SOUNDS TO ENGLISH-SPEAKING ears like "new hope," but it really means "we hope" in Haitian Creole, the language of the people who make up the "we" in the name of this non-profit. The origins of this organization began more than a decade ago through a relationship between a remote village in Haiti called LaMare and a family in the Midwest. It began when Richard and Sandy Doyle adopted three girls from the village. Through this adoption the Doyles' church and Melissa Millis, a college student at the time, began to travel back and forth to Haiti, cultivating a relationship with the local pastor and the people of the village.

Over time, the church became more and more involved and began to support a variety of community development initiatives in LaMare. Melissa and Sandy made several trips back and forth during those first years. They responded to the needs they saw, the needs that the pastor they worked with had identified. They did what they could to come alongside the Haitian people, helping make life more hopeful for them. Over time, the people of LaMare became more than just poor people in need of a helping hand from the West. They became real and dear to Melissa and Sandy. I had the good fortune to interview Melissa, and she described what has happened relationally over the last ten years as she traveled to Haiti.

These aren't just people to me. I've done life with them. I have a goddaughter there. They're family to me. To see them come out from underneath oppression—something so detrimental to who they are in Christ—affects me deeply. There's so much more to my relationship with them than me giving them something. They give me so much more. They have taught me what it looks like to have joy in the midst of deep and painful suffering. I've literally been given a bed, and they've slept on the dirt floor; I've been fed, and they haven't eaten that day.

In the beginning, however, it was a rough go for Sandy and Melissa. It took years for the villagers and leaders to trust them. As is often the case in the Haitian culture, instead of working directly with the people, they were obligated to work exclusively with the pastor of the village. Through his control of all incoming resources and their limited access to the people, fewer benefited from what they offered or were empowered to develop sustainable lives as families. As Melissa and Sandy began to realize this, it was a frustrating and disheartening realization. But at the time, they didn't totally understand why.

They finally came to the conclusion that some things needed to die, things that I will tell you about in chapter ten. So, after years of trying and not seeing the results they'd hoped for, Sandy and Melissa let go of their dream. They had no idea at the time if it was a permanent letting go or a temporary one. As you might suspect, it was temporary, and after four years of their dream lying dormant, this ministry to Haiti was "re-birthed" as Nou Hope.

As a result, they are seeing new hope emerge through providing the people of two villages, LaMare and Terre-Salei, with spiritual formation resources, educational training and community development. One of the most empowering endeavors to date is Nou Hope's support of a school where fifty women are learning to sew for a living and a group of men are making handcrafts. By establishing these small businesses, these villagers are developing a livelihood and boosting the local economy. In addition, Nou Hope has provided teacher's salaries, helped kids attend secondary schools, sent community leaders to the Global Leadership Summit and provided *Jesus Story Book Bibles* (Haitian Creole Version)—a way for them to learn the entire story of God and find their place in that story.

> We are at this new place of working with the entire community. We are doing things we've never done before. We're not only seeing the community come together in new ways—pushing toward a more sustainable future as they ground themselves in Christ—but we're also building relationships as we experience life together. For instance, we took the entire sixth-grade class to the Citadel—a fort occupied by the French and overturned when the slaves revolted and gained independence from France. All of the villagers know about this part of their history, but have never seen the fort, even though it's only about three hours away by truck.

From losing hope to rebirthing Nou Hope, Melissa and Sandy have had quite a journey realizing their God-given dream. It's been hard and discouraging at times, yet their passion never died. Now their vision has been revitalized as they see evidence of God's work through them accomplishing what they'd longed for—helping their Haitian friends overcome oppression and poverty and cultivate sustainable lives and growing faith.

10

DYING

*The seed must rest in the earth. We must allow the Christ-life
to grow in us in rest. Our whole being must fold upon
Christ's rest in us, as the earth folds upon the seed.*

Caryll Houselander

*F*OR THOSE WHO HAVE NEVER SUFFERED a miscarriage, it
might be hard to know what it's really like: the elusive emptiness, the hollow sorrow of losing something that you never held, something that never had visible substance, yet someone you had begun to
embrace. You'd found out that you were pregnant and soon your mind
was alive with images, with wonderment of what it would be like,
someday, to hold this little child in your arms. And when the miscarriage happened, all those dreams had nowhere to go, no funeral or place
to be buried.

For some, there are times during the gestation of a dream when you
begin to wonder if death is imminent. Your plans are on hold. You've
come to an impasse. The resources you need don't exist. All your energy's
been spent. You realize that there is nothing you can do, nothing at all,
to move things along or make happen what needs to happen to keep your
vision alive. As Richard Rohr put it, you've been "led to the edge of your
own private resources" and you know there is only One who holds the

lifeline and he seems, at present, to be unmoved.

For those who have actively nurtured a dream, it's heartbreaking to experience the death of that dream. You feel a similar elusive emptiness and hollow sorrow as those bereaved of a child—not the loss of a human life but the loss of a vision that had captured and consumed your imagination for months, maybe years, a dream in which you had invested time and thought and prayer and capital.

LETTING THINGS DIE

For Melissa Millis and Sandy Doyle, what appeared to be the death of their dream of serving the people of Haiti came after several years of investing themselves in this work.

> After seven years, there was a halting to what was being done. Among other things, we had been supporting teacher's salaries, but the lead pastor wanted all the money to come through him. We didn't want to do that anymore. We came to see that this whole thing we had envisioned of walking alongside the people became instead a way of supporting an oppressive leader. So we stopped. We had to let that part of our relationship die.

The vexing thing was that Melissa and Sandy had developed relationships with many of the people in community. They loved them. It was agonizing to feel like they were turning their backs on them. And yet they knew that they were at an impasse, that their support could never empower the people if they were confined to work through the current pastor.

So, for several years, neither Melissa nor Sandy went back to Haiti. It was a barren period for their dream. Melissa described her experience of this time:

> During the time of letting things die—go dormant—there was a deep sadness in me, a deep sadness that almost makes you feel sick to your stomach. You see people hurting; you see people not being

allowed to be who God intended them to be. You see the injustice of it. I felt an almost boiling rage inside me at times. How could this be happening? *God, how can you allow this to happen?*

Those are the questions we ask and the sickness we feel in our stomachs when we watch a dream we have nudged and nurtured, a dream we've given our hearts to, as it takes what looks like its final breaths. It is a great loss—a great loss indeed.

WHY SOME DREAMS NEED TO DIE

Why does this happen? What causes one dream to survive and another to miscarry? Just like in pregnancy, the answers are often a mystery. But right now it's important to ask a *different* question. Why might this dream *need* to die? What of significance might be happening through the dying process?

If you haven't figured it out by now, your pursuit of bringing this budding notion inside you to life is only partly about the dream and much about you, the dreamer. While all of the chapters thus far have described different stages in the development of a dream, and many of them had implications for you, the dreamer, this chapter on dying is about the deeper work that God is doing in you, the one in whom he has deposited this dream. So, again, what of significance might be happening *in you* through the dying process?

Jesus gave us a unique perspective on why things need to die when he said, "unless a grain of wheat falls into the earth and dies, it remains alone; but if it dies, it bears much fruit" (John 12:24 RSV). Jesus was using an analogy here. Of course, the meaning of his words foreshadow his own death and what his dying would accomplish for the whole human race. But if you know anything about a seed of grain, the true seed doesn't die, just the outer shell. When a seed falls to the ground and is covered by soil, the moist matter around it begins to work on the hard outer casement that protects the seed germ —the part of the seed that has reproductive capacities. Once that hard casement sloughs off, the true seed is able to sprout, shoot up through the soil, grow into a mature plant and bear fruit.

What dies is that which actually keeps the life-giving, fruit-producing potential of the true seed from being released. It originally served the purpose of protecting the seed, but now it has to die in order for the true seed to emerge—the seed that has the DNA, that has everything needed for the seed to grow into a healthy, mature, fruitful plant.

So, we might naturally want to ask, what of our dream must die in order for new potential to be released? When our dream goes through a period of dormancy or an actual dying process, it's possible that there are things about it that need to falter, to change and be sloughed off. It might have to do with how you are organizing or who you are working with, or where you want to plant it, or who the dream serves. Maybe things just need to slow down so that your vision is clearer or other resources can become available to you that are necessary for your new life, vocation or venture.

But oftentimes the dying process has more to do with *us* than the dream itself. So, the real question becomes, what *in us* must die in order for new potential to be released? We learn a lot about ourselves when we don't get what we want. Through the stress of losing what we have desired so much, we become acquainted with drives and compulsions that emerge because of our disappointment and experience of death. These are the character challenges that will ultimately inhibit our dream's fruitfulness. More importantly, these are the reactions and patterns that hinder us from being fully loving people, true and free, people who resemble Jesus.

During the lowest point of our journey, I felt that the death of our dream was imminent. I wrote in my journal,

> God has plopped himself down in the center of the path of our life as a stumbling stone. He is not budging. I think that death—death of our dream—is inevitable. It's okay. Do I want to be real? To be my true self enough to consent to die again? Yes, I hope so. I can kick against the goad or try to go around it, but it's useless. I choose to surrender. I choose to die.

I don't know that I *really* "chose" to die. I certainly struggled to consent to the dying process, and what came out of me was stubborn willfulness and drive—what I described in chapter nine. I chafed under the yoke of helplessness. I prayed incessantly and desperately, hoping that somehow God would cave under the pressure of my pleading. I tried everything in my power to get our house sold, including going to ridiculous lengths to make sure it was perfect for every showing. I also tried to finagle purchasing one particular property—trying to buy it before we sold ours. My actions revealed the desperateness and angst in my heart with being helpless and out of control. I resented God for prolonging the agony. "Hope deferred makes the heart sick," as the proverb goes (Proverbs 13:12). My heart was sick, and I anguished over having one so full of desire it could explode for a dream that appeared to be dying a slow death at my feet.

This quality of willfulness felt confusing too because it's so close in likeness to its cousin, perseverance, a quality that often serves me well. I wrote about my struggle with discerning the difference:

> I see a lot of willfulness and indignation when I'm not able to get what I want—to accomplish what I've set out to do. This willfulness in me is a double-edged sword. It serves me well when it comes to persevering amidst trials and challenges. It seems very necessary when it comes to initiating something like we are. So, when have I crossed the line, left or abandoned the yoke of Jesus and *pushed* my way forward?

When I looked at what was coming out of me it wasn't pretty. But it was also really important for me to see and acknowledge before God and to myself. I've found that when life is easy and unruffled, I function fairly well. I come to realize the truth of my spiritual condition under pressure and the stress of losing control. That's where, through death, God has an advantage. Again, as Rohr put it, "This is the only way that Life-Fate-God-Grace-Mystery can get you to change, let go of your egocentric preoccupations, and go the further and larger journey." I do want to change. I do want to go the further and larger journey, and so this Via

Dolorosa is a necessary passage. The seed must fall to the ground and die for the potential of the true seed to emerge.

You may discover as I did that the logistics of what need to happen to realize your vision are less important to God than the work he desires to do in you. Death, as hard as it is, is a chance to pause, to rest, to put activity on hold and pay attention to the inner work of God. As Caryll Houselander wrote, "The seed must rest in the earth. We must allow the Christ-life to grow in us in rest. Our whole being must fold upon Christ's rest in us, as the earth folds upon the seed." So, rather than see death as an end or a failure, something to work feverishly to avoid, it can be a time of sloughing off what isn't you in order for the Christ in you to emerge.

REFLECTION: PAYING ATTENTION TO WHAT'S HAPPENING THROUGH THE DYING PROCESS

You will undoubtedly feel a sense of great loss if you happen to go through the death of a dream or experience a period of dormancy when it looks like your dream is dying. If you experience setbacks—small and large "deaths"—one of your most important tasks is to pay attention to what is going on inside you and what is coming out of you. As we pay attention to the egotistical strategies of our false self, it is important to extend hospitality to them so that we can learn more about them and expose them to the light of Christ's love as we grow into our true self.

So, stop for a moment and take an inventory of what you are noticing.

- What are you noticing that is happening inside you through the setbacks you have experienced?

- What patterns or reactions are coming out of you? Describe them honestly, with raw language.

- What do you know about these patterns and reactions? Do they come from shame, fear or anger? Have you seen them before? What are the life situations that often prompt them?

- How do you feel toward God right now? How are you experiencing him? What images do you have of him during this time of dormancy or death?

- Take some time to meditate on and visualize the chapter's epigraph: "The seed must rest in the earth. We must allow the Christ-life to grow in us in rest. Our whole being must fold upon Christ's rest in us, as the earth folds upon the seed."

- In prayer, imagine yourself "resting in the earth." Open yourself to the Christ life growing in you; imagine your whole being folding upon his rest in you.

INTERVIEW

*Suzy Roth and Hands of Hope Adoption
and Orphan Care Ministry*

FROM A YOUNG AGE SUZY ROTH had an unusual and tender heart for God, as well as a sensitive conscience toward the things that are on God's heart. One day, during high school, she was reading the book of James and came across the verse "Pure and genuine religion in the sight of God the Father means caring for orphans and widows in their distress and refusing to let the world corrupt you" (James 1:27). It was as though the words jumped off the page at her. Suzy began to wonder what they meant—caring for orphans and widows. Though she wouldn't have called it a dream at the time, that day a seed was planted which later grew into a God-given dream.

Now, fast forward several years: Suzy had graduated from college, had begun a career, married her husband, Kevin, and become the mother of three kids.

Nothing had happened with that seed for a long time. Well, actually, life happened. Then there was a slight reawakening—a little watering—when a good friend of ours adopted a child from South Korea. That event made me think about the verse again. *Maybe this is what we could do; rather than* have *a fourth child we could* adopt *a fourth.*

Suzy shared her prompting with Kevin, and they both agreed to take a year and pray about it. At the time, Suzy was the more open of the two; it appeared that Kevin might require a bit more convincing. But after a year was up, they had a conversation and it was obvious that Kevin's heart had changed. So, they moved forward in mid-January with an adoption agency, hoping to adopt a child from Russia. And by mid-March they were on their way to Russia to meet and bring home their son, Jonathan. Two months—an unprecedented time for an adoption to go through!

At this point, Suzy felt that her openness to adopt was more from a sense of obedience. That was until she and Kevin arrived at the orphanage where they would meet baby Jonathan. They pulled up to the building on a dreary, wintery day and Suzy witnessed a scene that has never left her memory.

> When I saw these children standing outside in the cold—no playground, nothing to do, just standing there in the parking lot because there was snow everywhere—I couldn't get over it. They had to be taken outside because of a problem with rickets (caused by not enough exposure to sunlight). They were really just *standing* there. That was the image that was seared in my mind.

Even still, Suzy would not call the tug on her heart to respond to this need to "take care of orphans" a God-given dream. It seemed overwhelming to consider, now with four kids six and under. Then, about a year later, Suzy was at an event for small group leaders at her church and the facilitator at her table posed a question: "So, if you could realize any dream, what would it be?" One by one, they went around the table and people gave words to their dreams. When it came to Suzy, she described her dream to care for orphans and to help adoptive families.

> I think that was the first time I said it out loud. I shared it but honestly thought it was a pipe dream. I couldn't do anything with it at that time. I just thought it would be cool to do. After adopting Jonathan and my experience at the orphanage, the desire never left.

Maybe the desire was in me, but I didn't know it until I spoke it. I felt sadness after that, discouraged because of my desire and inability to act. I saw no path forward with it. I didn't even see the next step. I really believe, though, that *that* was the moment the dream was born.

Four years passed and it seemed that the birth of her dream had either miscarried, died or lay frozen in time. Then one day, Suzy met another woman from her church with the same heart and vision. That seemed to be the missing element—the spur that Suzy needed to take action! Finding a partner helped her channel her energy and passion toward cultivating a now shared dream.

From there, we got a core group who were committed to the vision, and they eventually became the board of directors of Hands of Hope Adoption and Orphan Care Ministry. I've never felt like I was on my own. There've been others praying, sharing ideas, joining in—that's been huge. From the get-go, we've had a team around us.

Since that time, and to date, Hands of Hope has raised just under $200,000 for assistance to adoptive families and has helped place twenty-six children from thirteen countries into loving homes. They sponsor a yearly conference called Starting Points, a day-long conference that helps people learn about the greatest areas of need in adoption today, and prepares them to adopt. They also help connect families who are interested in adoption with families who have adopted. In addition to their adoption services, Hands of Hope helps resource and support six nontraditional orphanages and children's homes, five international and one domestic.

One of the first services Hands of Hope offered early on were informational gatherings for people interested in adoption. At one of those meetings, a woman came—someone Suzy doesn't recall meeting. A few years later, Suzy was in the lobby of the church when this woman approached her with two children at her side. "A woman came up to me and introduced herself. She said that she had come to one of the informational meetings and because of what she learned there, she wanted to introduce me to the two children she adopted." Suzy couldn't believe it! She felt absolutely humbled and speechless. Her eyes overflowed with tears as she saw what had been an unknown impact of her God-given dream.

Suzy reflected, "This has been one of the great privileges of my life. It's been incredible to see God's hand on this ministry and the children who have benefited. He opens doors before I know they need to be open. God is always one step ahead."

11

RESURRECTING

When the time is right, the cocooned soul begins to emerge. Waiting turns golden. Newness unfurls. It's a time of pure, unmitigated wonder. Yet as we enter the passage of emergence, we need to remember that new life comes slowly, awkwardly, on wobbly wings.

Sue Monk Kidd

*O*N WEDNESDAY, APRIL 25, 2012, the "Most-Moved-Mover" removed the stone that obstructed the realization of our dream. After the long and exhausting experience of showing our home seventy-two times over eight months, on this date we received two offers. The first came in the morning; the second, who knew about the first, came in the afternoon. Offer number two was a full-price offer.

Our waiting had turned golden. Like a butterfly emerging from the dark tomb of her cocoon, our dream, in what felt like an instant, unfurled her wings. We were overcome with gratefulness and unmitigated wonder. Resurrection! Yet, truthfully, we moved forward, embracing our revived dream cautiously, awkwardly, with wobbly wings.

My first impulse was to tell God how sorry I was for not trusting him, to grovel in shame at my lack of faith and frustration with his timing. Through the grueling process, I had become depressed and despondent. Then suddenly, the thing that we felt would never happen happened. I was instantly humbled and enormously thankful, relieved and amazed at the grace of it.

Once we felt relatively confident that the offer was good and the necessary steps to sell our home were in motion, we began to look for this unique property we had envisioned. As I mentioned earlier, we had our eye on a few places, but by this time they had all sold. We went back to the Internet and studied all that we could find on the market in our price range and the area where we hoped to live . . . and nothing, absolutely nothing, showed up that met our criteria.

Two anxious weeks passed and we began to wonder if we would have to move into temporary housing or settle for something that was less than ideal. Compromise was such a disappointing consideration after having come this far. Finally, we changed the property specifications of our online search and an interesting new listing showed up. As I looked over the description, the first two floors had adequate space and room sizes, and it had an *unfinished* third floor. So, on a rainy Tuesday morning, my dear friend and realtor, Pam, walked with David and me onto the expansive porch of a hundred-year-old home, through the front door, and into a space that I immediately sensed had the "X factor"—that serene, stately, gracious, sacred DNA we were looking for. We pretty much knew instantly that we had come home.

DON'T GIVE UP!

If you have been moving through the gestational process of bringing a dream to life, and that dream has appeared to die or at least be in "sleep saver" mode, it can be hard to keep hope alive. I believe that many who have given birth to a dream would like to say to you, in unison, "Don't give up!" Just because at this moment in time your dream appears to be lifeless, don't assume that what you have desired and pursued will not, at some future moment, be revived. Keep your eyes open for the unfolding evidence of resurrection.

The second thing that you need to know (if you've hit this wall or are at this point) is that as much as the initial pursuit of a dream requires risk, reviving a dream that's gone dormant can feel even riskier. If you've exerted a ton of effort toward an unfulfilled dream, it's possible that you aren't sure you have it in you to go another round. You might struggle now with trusting your own judgment because of a previously failed attempt to do what was in your heart. The thought of failing a second time is too humiliating to stomach. Along with all this are the haunting whispers of self-doubt that can erase any optimism or confidence you once had.

Even when you begin to notice that God may be reviving your dream, rather than elation, you might feel some ambivalence. For instance, if the obstacle that had kept you from pursuing your dream is suddenly removed, you may feel both excitement and anxiety. This mixture of emotions can be confusing and create even more uncertainty, like some who have gone through a divorce and are considering remarriage—their desire and trepidation can be undoing.

During the passage from death to life, as Sue Monk Kidd reminds us, "we need to remember that new life comes slowly, awkwardly, on wobbly wings." In other words, hang in there, even if you feel clumsy and hesitant as you witness the potential resurrection of your once listless dream. Wait it out and keep your eyes open for what God is doing.

FINDING MARY

Perhaps each of us who have experienced the death and dawning resurrection of a dream need our own unique confirmation, and that will come in different forms. For Suzy Roth, it came in the form of learning that someone else in her church had a similar vision as she. One day, Suzy lamented to her husband, Kevin, who was one of the pastors of her church, that she continued to feel a stirring in her heart to start a ministry to support orphans and adoptive families—but felt a deep sadness at not knowing where to begin.

I thought about it all the time, but it didn't fit my life. I didn't have any ideas of how to do it. The dream felt buried because I couldn't see any way forward. There were too many barriers. It didn't seem feasible. I felt the sense that this would be a great thing to do and a deep sadness for the orphans, but didn't know what to do.

Then Kevin responded by telling her that he had just heard about another woman in their church who had the same desire. When Suzy heard this, her heart suddenly felt light. It was the nudge she needed to take the next, pivotal step. Perhaps it confirmed that her perceptions of the need were real and from God. Perhaps it sparked the courage and stimulus she needed to move forward. So, Suzy initiated with this woman, Mary, and together, through their shared energy and zeal, plans began to take shape; they began to develop a shared vision for Hands of Hope.

We got together and started to brainstorm and talk about how we could do this together. Mary and her husband were in the process of an international adoption. I had no grand vision for this. I didn't even have anything specific other than getting people together to talk about it. So, we identified a broader group of people to bring together to brainstorm—people who had adopted, both domestic and international. It was a leap of faith, a next step—but totally not knowing the step after that. Finding Mary was huge for me! Together we thought, *Let's take this jump and see where God leads us!*

Finding another person to partner with was a significant moment for Suzy, and may have been the resurrection sign she needed to step out and realize her long-considered and slow-to-come dream. Since the time, way back in high school, when Suzy had begun to dream her dream, one of the issues that she had struggled with was her own sense of inadequacy. She was a leader but never felt like a visionary or the kind of person to give birth to a dream of this scope. Bless God, who knew and accepted this about Suzy and provided a co-conspirator who would partner with her, bringing another voice, experience and skills to the table. "Finding Mary was huge" for Suzy and gave her the courage and needed companionship to believe that her dream had risen; it was indeed alive and ready to be embraced.

Suzy shared with me what she finally came to realize after all this time:

> I often thought, *I'm just not the right person to lead this. I don't have all the skill sets.* Yet, I finally came to realize that nobody has all the skills. So, I will just have to find people who can fill in the gaps. Yes, I am inadequate. I don't have it all. But this is where God wants me and so I'm going to be faithful.

NOTICING THE SIGNS OF RESURRECTION

Consider the experiences of Jesus' disciples when they were confronted with his resurrection. You would think that they all would have been overjoyed. Yet the Gospel accounts describe each one struggling to believe, guardedly considering the evidence and filled with a combination of amazement and cautiousness. Each one became convinced of Jesus' resurrection through an encounter with unique signs of life.

- The female disciples experienced an earthquake causing the stone of Jesus' tomb to roll away, an angelic presence announced that Jesus was alive and they had a face-to-face encounter with him. (Matthew 28:1-10)

- Peter and John saw the empty tomb and castoff grave clothes and believed. (John 20:3-10)

- The two disciples walking together on a road to Emmaus experienced their hearts burn and eyes open as Jesus revealed the Scriptures and broke bread with them. (Luke 24:13-34)

- A large gathering of disciples were in an upper room hiding from the Jewish authorities when Jesus materialized before them and showed them his hands and side. (John 20:19-23)

- Thomas said he wouldn't believe until he could see Jesus for himself, touch his side and nail-pierced hands—and Jesus invited him to do just that. (John 20:24-29)

For those of us whose dreams appear to have died, there will be signs of life that signal and convince us of resurrection—but it can be a slow dawning, one that feels tenuous and shaky. It's important to be attentive to the signs of life. The following questions will help you pay attention and name any confirming evidence that life, indeed, has returned to your dream.

REFLECTION: SIGNS OF LIFE

1. What circumstances, both external and internal, led you to lay down your dream for a time, to believe that it was either in a period of dormancy or had died?

2. What signs of life cause you to wonder if God is resurrecting your dream?

3. What obstacles, if any, have been removed?

4. What doors, if any, have been opened?

5. How do you feel about reengaging your dream?

6. Who can you talk with about your feelings and what you're observing? Whose counsel might you seek? Have you shared your musings with your spiritual director (if you have one)?

Part Three

BIRTHING A
GOD-GIVEN DREAM

INTERVIEW

Tom Durant and Eco Café Haiti

*T*HOUGH HE WAS FIFTY YEARS OLD, Tom Durant had a childlike faith. He had been raised in a Christian home, but as a young adult Tom abandoned his Christian roots in pursuit of other things. And though he experienced tremendous success in those other things—as a businessman and entrepreneur—Tom recognized at this midpoint of his life that something was missing. He felt compelled to reengage his childhood faith and seek to know Christ as an adult. During that time, the pastor of Tom's church began to meet regularly with him and pour his life into Tom's. Tom got excited as he saw his faith growing and seeping into his conversations and relationships. He was surprised to notice that others were actually receptive when he shared his faith. Tom's desire for God to use him and his belief that there was more God wanted of and for him intensified. He just didn't know how.

Tom expressed this desire to his pastor, who gave him books to read about missions. What Tom had yet to realize was that God could use Tom's own leadership and entrepreneurial skills to collaborate in God's kingdom work in the world by empowering others who were oppressed through economic poverty.

Tom explained, "I had to overcome this worldview that I had; it was somewhat jaded. It was that economic development was in conflict with my faith. The more I studied the Bible and became aware, the more comfortable I felt. Maybe this is my calling in my life."

One of the books Tom read was called *The Great Commission Company: The Emerging Role of Business in Mission.* This was an awakening for him. In it Tom read about how important economic development is to underdeveloped countries. One example was about a company who helped farmers in Costa Rica live sustainable lives through growing and exporting fair trade coffee beans. That appealed to Tom, and a similar business model began to emerge in his entrepreneurial mind.

> I had started businesses before. So, I had confidence. I had traveled a lot too. I had the background. I just had never focused on an underdeveloped country. And I had no idea about coffee! I simply looked at my purpose to create a money-making enterprise to help an economically depressed country. It was later that the feeding of the poor and the sustaining of the environment evolved.

He began to understand that the best gifts he had to offer God were his gifts and experience as a businessman. But he had no idea where to begin. Then one day, as Tom was passing by the refrigerator in his kitchen, he noticed the picture of little girl—a Haitian girl that he had been supporting for some time. He thought to himself, *Why not Haiti?* So, he went online and started searching for organizations that were doing work in Haiti. He came across Christian Flights International, and contacted the director. When Tom shared with this man what he was interested in doing, the director said, "That's amazing! We just abandoned our agriculture initiative for lack of funds." Tom made a trip to Haiti, formed an alliance with CFI and eventually raised funds through them until Eco Café Haiti was established as a nonprofit.

Once Tom got started, "way led to way"—as it so often does. His original and singular vision was to provide the training and resources for the Haitians in the village of Ranquitte to develop a livelihood by growing and exporting coffee beans. But as he tried to explain this to the farmers in Ranquitte, he ran into a bit of a glitch. "Try to explain the coffee enterprise to Haitians. They couldn't understand. All they wanted was something that would provide for their immediate needs—hunger. So, we incentivized by providing seeds for food."

Once he recognized and addressed the immediate need of hunger, Tom's vision also expanded to healing the environment. As Tom traveled about Haiti, he witnessed firsthand the heavily deforested land and its effect on the environment. A third prong was added to the mission of Eco Café Haiti—a mission to enable economic self-sufficiency in rural Haiti by cultivating, processing and exporting quality Haitian coffee, to cultivate land for growing food, and to restore the heavily deforested ecological environment to good health.

Tom has invested his talents and is experiencing the reward and seeing encouraging results. However, none of the reward for him is financial—it all goes back into the community and enterprises. As the founder of the organization, Tom receives no remuneration for his services. Eco Café Haiti is a Haitian employee-owned company, the benefits of which accrue solely to the Haitian employees and the community of Ranquitte.

Tom shared his reflections on his journey of birthing this God-given dream:

> I wouldn't have embarked on this dream if I hadn't sensed God was in it. I began to look back over my life and now this dream makes a lot of sense. All these things have sculpted me to do this very thing. In retrospect, as I look at every twist and turn, I see God's providence in it.

12

BIRTHING

This is no time for a child to be born,
With the earth betrayed by war and hate
And a comet slashing the sky to warn
That time runs out and the sun burns late.

That was no time for a child to be born,
In a land in the crushing grip of Rome;
Honour and truth were trampled by scorn—
Yet here did the Saviour make his home.

When is the time for love to be born?
The inn is full on the planet earth,
And by a comet the sky is torn—
Yet Love still takes the risk of birth.

Madeleine L'Engle

EVERY DAY, APPROXIMATELY **370,000** babies are born around the world—370,000 miracles! For many, there's something about the birth of a baby that gets us every time. How is it that most of them form so perfectly? How is it that we humans have the outlandish ability and privilege to procreate? Each new life reminds us that Love still takes the risk of birth, still hangs in there with us, the human race, not giving up on us or abandoning us or leaving us to our own devises. God comes to us, again and again, through each little child born in each particular manger, bearing the God image from the moment of his or her conception and revealed at his or her birth.

Just as the birth of babies stuns us into conscious awareness of the reality of God—of something that is beyond us and for us—so, I believe, the birth of small, creative, outlandish endeavors remind us that God still takes the risk of birth. God longs to procreate with us through inspired kingdom initiatives. In Zechariah 4:10, an angel said to Zechariah, "Do not despise these small beginnings, for the LORD rejoices to see the work begin." Today is that day, the day of the birth of a dream, the day of small beginnings.

THE DAY OF SMALL BEGINNINGS

Through my interviews and interactions with people in my community and from around the country, I'm aware that God is up to something in these small beginnings. I notice a trend where countless individuals are feeling the nudge of God to give birth to small things. These aren't typically large world-changing megabusinesses, corporations, organizations or churches. They are infant-size initiatives, often with a small reach. What I sense is that God is in this day of small endeavors, and perhaps through these micro-initiatives, he is weaving a web of care that will span the globe.

Small has captured me. In the past, I've been part of large organizations and megachurches. During those times, much of my energy was given to "big." I worked hard to create large venues and gatherings, spoke at and organized those venues where large portions of resources were invested. Not so now. I am investing my life quietly, in the small, in the few.

A couple of years ago I received an email from a friend, Rob Loane. He works alongside Randy Reese with VantagePoint3. At the end of his email, he had, as part of his signature, a quote by Rufus Jones, a nineteenth-century Quaker. It read, "I pin my hopes on the quiet processes and small circles in which vital and transforming events take place." After the first time I read it, I found myself returning to the email just to re-read the end quote. I realized that it expressed for me the shift within myself, the change from serving the big to serving the small—believing in the small, pinning my hopes on the small.

If you are one who is giving birth to a dream, large or small, don't diminish the day of small beginnings. Remember that Jesus came to us in the small, tender form of a baby, as do all of the 370,000 miracles born each day. Don't underplay the significance of the day your dream is born. Work with the labor to bring it forward, this brainchild of God and yours. Celebrate it and dedicate it to the Love that still takes the risk of birth.

CELEBRATING BIG MOMENTS

Though many of the dreams people seem to be impassioned to birth are of a smallish variety, it is important, just the same, to celebrate big moments in those small endeavors. For some, celebrating and acknowledging milestones is natural, an expression of their particular bent. Tom Durant would tell you he doesn't happen to be one of those naturals. Tom is an entrepreneur. And by nature, entrepreneurs are driven by the fact that, though much has been accomplished, there's so much more to be done! And pressing on would be Tom's bent.

However, since founding Eco Café Haiti, Tom has learned the importance of celebrating those big moments and milestones that are important to everyone involved in giving birth to a dream—including him! Tom recalls a couple of significant moments of celebration during those initial months:

> It took twelve months of planning just to amass all the supplies, equipment and building materials needed for our coffee mill, all of which had to be exported to Haiti, exported from Brazil, Colombia and the United States. In Haiti, it is very difficult to find or purchase the items that go into making a coffee mill, a total of over three hundred line items. It took another three months to organize

the logistics of shipping containers carrying our goods to Cap-Haïtien. Finally, it took three weeks of daily negotiation with Haitian customs and taxation officials to release our cargo: fees, as they would say; bribes, as defined by any other. When all was said and done, the facility was operational and ready for our first crop. We celebrated the event with a glass of clarin, the unrefined and partially distilled version of Haitian rum, a ghastly concoction that did not settle well with any of us, particularly those who don't drink.

The second moment of note was the day in which our Hawaiian coffee agronomist, Dan Kuhn, cupped our coffee for the first time. The cupping process is an elaborate event in which the coffee is religiously roasted, measured, brewed and tasted, an event that to the aficionado is akin to a rite of sacrament, a very holy event requiring strict adherence to each step in the process. When Dan Kuhn first cupped our coffee and declared that it was "Very good. Indeed very, very good," I was elated. Our Haitian employees who witnessed the event broke out in riotous laughter, laughter over the way in which Dan slurped the coffee in his mouth "to fill all taste buds in the palate," as Dan would say, slurping that produced a very odd sound similar to a wet-dry vacuum sucking up spilled water.

Those were some initial big moments that remain in Tom's scrapbook of memories, moments that he and others took time to mark through celebration. He also shared with me during his interview that for the past couple of years, he has continued to celebrate important accomplishments through an annual awards ceremony. "Each year, for the last few years, we have an awards ceremony for the farmers. We give awards for the farmers who have grown the most coffee, bonuses for the employees who have been with us longest or worked the hardest."

It's becoming a part of the culture of Eco Café Haiti to acknowledge what has been accomplished, not only noticing what is still left to do. Though Tom might chide himself as one who doesn't let up on the accelerator easily, an entrepreneur who is never quite satisfied with the

results of his endeavors, he is establishing a best practice of commemo-
rating and celebrating what God has done through the combined efforts
of many.

NATURAL DREAM BIRTHING

I will never forget lying in a hospital bed, preparing to give birth to our
first child. I was hooked up to an IV of pitocin, a drug used to induce
labor, listening to a woman in the next room in active labor. The sound
coming from her was petrifying! I listened, thinking to myself, *Is that
going to be me?*

I never saw her, but I pictured her. Her loud, guttural screams made
me suspect she was a large, robust woman with a set of humongous lungs.
Every time she had a contraction, it sounded like she gripped the sides
of her bed and fought them with all her might, as if by doing so she could
get them to stop. I listened, vowing to myself that I would try a different
approach.

I had planned to give birth naturally. In that moment, I realized that
I could either work *with* the contractions or *against* them. I could allow
them to do their work or fight the work they were trying to do by re-
sisting them. I won't tell you that I followed through on my vow with
flawless execution. I did succeed in squeezing the circulation from my
husband's hand in an effort to not scream my head off.

If you have conceived a God-given dream, the moment you have been
waiting for is the birth of that dream. Birth comes when you move in,
open the doors, hang the sign, board the plane, launch the website or do
whatever it is you do to inaugurate the tangible beginning of this thing
that you have been incubating for untold months or years. Like any birth,
there will be surprises. Similar to parents of a newborn, you may find
yourself thinking, *This is exactly what I thought it would be like.* But more
probable, you will, at times think, *This is nothing like what I expected!*

Birthing a dream is an exciting adventure with a fulfilling end—at
least for many. The moment of birth is when the intangible becomes
tangible, when what you had sketched on paper actually becomes a con-

crete entity. So, what do you need to know about natural dream birthing?

First, work with the Spirit's movement, not against it. As labor progresses and you realize that your dream has an opening date on the calendar, don't get ahead of or lag behind the work. Many find this to be a real art. Whether you are a "J" or "P" on the Myers-Briggs Type Indicator might determine which direction is more of a challenge. In short—Js tend to get ahead; Ps tend to lag behind. But the important thing is to monitor the labor. Keep aligned with the natural current or progress of the birth.

So, how do you do that? Let's refer back to a concept I introduced in chapter ten on waiting. Margaret Silf, through the lens of Ignatian spirituality, described the way it feels to be in sync or out-of-sync with God. She said, "The action of God on our lives is always, at its heart, experienced as a drawing. If we are feeling driven, then the prompting that gives rise to it is not from God but from the force fields of our own (or other people's) kingdoms."

Pay attention to the way you are accomplishing the things that need to be done, to the energy of your movement. Are you pushing forward or being carried along? Being carried is not effortless and will require work on your part, but it is participatory work—work with the Spirit. It will feel more like being in the flow than forced labor. That's the natural Spirit-led way to birth a dream.

Another important element is to take time to bond with your new venture. Slow down enough to savor the beginning. Use your senses to take in all that is new and exciting, as well as those things that feel scary or awkward, or even a loss. Embrace the moment of your dream's birth and appreciate what it is—the miracle of it!

When we moved into our home and retreat center, both David and I found ourselves, several times a day, noticing the gift of it. Often, a wave of gratefulness would wash over me as I became aware of just how perfect this place was for us and for the purposes God had instilled in our hearts. As I used the space and got used to it, organized life in it and through it, I continued to marvel over the way it fit our needs. I bonded with our home, and on numerous occasions had to simply stop where I was and thank God for his goodness, wisdom and grace toward us in leading us to it.

So, do take time to bond with the new life you have birthed, whether it be a new vocation, move to the city or country, or a nonprofit or creative business venture. Take time to make it your own. Receive it as a gift.

Next, once you've actually moved in, are up and running, and are living your dream, don't forget to celebrate it. Can you imagine a couple giving birth to a baby and then going about their lives, business as usual? Don't forget to take time to revel in where you have been and what has transpired. Chronicle your journey, take pictures, keep a journal or album, start a Facebook page, commemorate what has happened, send out a "birth" announcement!

These notes will help you remember all the ways that God was with you and for you, how he has led you along the journey. Countless times the Israelites were instructed to remember the ways God led them out of captivity and into the Promised Land. "Remember how the LORD your God led you through the wilderness for these forty years, humbling you and testing you to prove your character, and to find out whether or not you would obey his commands" (Deuteronomy 8:2). These acts and memories are part of your sacred story. They are just as significant as the stories of others in Scripture who have been led along by God to bring to life an expression of the kingdom of God. So remember and celebrate! And invite others to celebrate with you!

Finally, dedicate your dream to God. We can observe such great traditions in the Old Testament of the practice of dedicating—babies, days, significant events, land, tabernacles and temples—to the Lord. What might it look like for you to dedicate your dream to God for his purposes? Perhaps you might want to write a dedication and hang it somewhere for you and others to see. This plaque will be a reminder of your commitment to honor God and the purposes of this dream he has given you and helped you realize. Or maybe you want to create a "contract" that outlines the commitments you are making to maintain the integrity of what you are doing and who you are serving. Maybe you need to host a gathering of your friends and have them pray over you and the space you occupy or the plan you have laid out.

Whatever you do, mark the birth of your dream with both celebration and dedication. Don't wait till everything is perfect or running without a glitch. From the start, whether it is a "soft" opening or a full-fledged "we're open for business," signify this moment in a significant and meaningful way for yourself and all those who have been involved in this dream.

One of the ways we have continuously celebrated our dream is through a constant flow of people we have invited over to see and experience Sustainable Faith Indy. Typically, we take them on a tour and tell them our story. We explain what we want our place to be for them and others. We sit down, and over coffee, tea or a glass of wine we engage them in conversation so that they can experience our values—hospitality, presence, conversation and contemplative living. In the course of our first year, it's quite possible that we hosted over six hundred family members, old friends and new friends through individual meetings and as part of groups. We wasted no time stepping into this dream and living it with all our heart and soul.

REFLECTION: IDEAS TO CELEBRATE AND DEDICATE YOUR DREAM

Take some time to brainstorm how you might celebrate and dedicate the birth of your dream. Be creative and generate a list of several ideas. Then look over your calendar and schedule a time when the celebration and dedication can happen!

INTERVIEW

Katie Taylor and Film School Africa

ATIE TAYLOR WAS LIVING HER DREAM and the dream of many who aspire to work in the film industry in Hollywood. She had been working in this movie-making culture for a number of years, working hard, watching doors open and seeing impressive success. Then a different kind of door opened—one that led her down a path and in a direction that she hadn't anticipated.

Katie gave a little background:

> I was working with a couple of executive producers, was part of the Writers Guild of America and then had shifted into some amazing jobs in casting for some big films. I had a lot of success. I saw some big doors opening to me. For a really long time my passion was about exposing Hollywood to Christians and Christians to Hollywood. Then, in 2005, I went to South Africa on a mission's trip, to the Kayamandi Township.

Katie experienced sensory shock, leaving the opulent surroundings and sophistication of Hollywood and entering the world of abject poverty within this South African township—a one square mile plot of land occupied by forty thousand black South Africans. Townships had been established during apartheid to keep black people separate from white people. During her trip, Katie volunteered with a photography ministry.

(You guessed it—the Viewfinder Project!) They went into homes, took a picture of the family, prayed for them and then returned later with a framed copy of the picture. She had an incredible time, but no idea what it would mean to her later.

> About six months later, I was sitting and listening to a talk at a singles' ministry and all of a sudden I had this idea for a film, and I started writing it down. My visions come to me in pictures and images. I'm not the kind of person who usually says, "God said . . ." But it was clear God was speaking to me. So, I started writing, and before you know it, I'd written the screenplay for a short film. But I knew I would have to go back to South Africa to film it.

And so she did, a second time.

> We shot this movie in about a day and a half with no budget. It's about a little girl who is losing everybody because of HIV. I had once heard it said that in America the face of HIV is a homosexual man. Around the world, it's often a young woman or girl. Throughout the film, this girl talks about all the people she is losing to HIV. In the end, the people she says she's losing are actually the ones lowering her into the grave because she's lost her life to HIV.

Katie had an amazing experience directing this short film, and when she returned to Hollywood her mind kept returning to the experience, as if the memory was haunting her. Finally, a plan came together in her mind. She had a lot of questions and didn't have all the answers, but sensed God nudging her to discover a way to use film—an industry that is booming in South Africa—to bring healing and hope for those in Kayamandi.

Over the next several months, Katie wrote a curriculum to teach film to students, and made plans to return to South Africa—this time for six months. She started a film class in the township, and thirteen students joined her first class. Those six months were life-changing.

It was the process of getting to know the students that changed me. We began an ongoing documentary about their lives. Part of the process was them sitting with me, talking with me while the camera was rolling. That gave me a good excuse to push in and ask the questions that no one was asking. That created an incredible bond with me and them. They were really open. I didn't know if they would be.

Through teaching the course, Katie discovered that some of the students caught on really fast and developed amazing skills. Each student created his or her own short film, and as part of graduation they had a red carpet ceremony. "They walked the red carpet, and then we showed their films. I saw them come alive! They just beamed! I knew from that point on, anything I did in Hollywood would pale. I felt for the first time that I was using all the gifts and talents God had given me."

At the end of six months, and after a tearful goodbye, Katie returned home. A deep connection had been formed between her and the students, one that she couldn't ignore and refused to neglect. Katie went to work to figure out how to return, full-time. It took a lot of work and commitment, but eventually it paid off, and Katie moved to South Africa and founded a nonprofit called Film School Africa.

Here's how Katie explains her vision:

My goal is to use the power of storytelling to create jobs and life-sustaining change in individuals. I work with high school students and beyond, teaching them the skills of screenwriting, camera work, editing and directing actors. We have photography courses for children 8-18. We teach poetry and hip-hop writing, using film-making and all the surrounding art forms to equip students to develop the life skills to get a job. We also use film as a form of art therapy. We use storytelling to help students work through trauma. We are harnessing the power of film to forever change lives.

13

LIVING

We do not think ourselves into a new way of living;
but we live ourselves into a new way of thinking.

Richard Rohr

*S*O YOUR DREAM HAS BECOME A REALITY. Now what?

That's often a question people ask, consciously or unconsciously, once they've accomplished a significant, long-attended goal like running a marathon or finishing a degree or giving birth to a dream. Suddenly there's no hill to climb, no big event to plan for or work toward.

If or when you accomplish what you set out to do, you may begin to wonder how to keep your energy flowing and your momentum going. You might even feel a significant letdown. Maybe living your dream is close to what you expected or even better than you expected. Sometimes, though, it's different and challenging. There are adjustments at every turn. What you're beginning to experience is your "new normal."

YOUR NEW NORMAL

Your new normal involves all those things that are different from your old way of doing life. It can include new things that you see every day that you didn't use to see—things that are beautiful and things that are disorienting. Your new normal can involve new habits that are required of you. Perhaps your dream demands that you be in the "office" at 8 a.m. Or maybe that was part of your former life and your new normal is to work from home and have no set schedule to keep. Both are challenging adjustments. Your new normal can also involve opportunities where you will need to grow—your growing edge, as I will talk about in a bit. There may be skills or capacities that your new work and life require of you. You will have to "grow into them."

After we had lived in our home for a couple of months, I made a list of several things that were part of my "new normal." Here are a few that I came up with:

- We take walks or ride bikes most days and encounter the disparate mix of beauty and poverty: quaint, well-manicured homes and a homeless man sleeping under a bridge, the striking skyline of our city along the Cultural Trail and the sight of abandoned houses and trash littering the streets.

- We shop at stores that are unfamiliar and different and remind me that I'm not in Fishers (our former suburb) any more.

- We live in a one-hundred-year-old home with wide doorways and ten-foot ceilings, with creaks and sighs and stories to tell.

- We (occasionally) still search for light switches, open the door to the closet thinking it's the bathroom and forget which direction to turn for the microwave.

- We set a security alarm when we leave and when we go to bed.

- We spend more time staying than going—welcoming people into our new home who are curious about what we're doing, interested in spiritual direction or coming for a retreat, or inquisitive friends who want to see our new "digs."

- We walk about with deep, overflowing joy in our hearts for how God has blessed us and for how glad we are to be on this adventure together.

If we initiate something as significant as a new life dream, it will change our lives. It's important to become aware of and acknowledge the differences from the way life was, maybe even make a list of them, as I did. But the only way to truly embrace the new normal is to *live* into it. I love the epigraph by Richard Rohr at the beginning of the chapter: "We do not think ourselves into a new way of living; but we live ourselves into a new way of thinking."

This profound and insightful statement goes against the grain of how we typically try to think our way through transition and change. Living your way means engaging in movement; choosing to act, feel, taste, touch, smell, respond and react to life in your new world or new responsibilities. A cautious and calculated approach won't do. Holding back from the challenges or withdrawing from the difficulties will only serve to imprison you in the fear of failure. Once you've given birth to your dream, it's time to live into that dream, full out and full on!

One of the living full-out and full-on stories I heard about during my interviews was with Katie Taylor; she had to live her way into a very new and very different normal—one of stark contrast to her prior life.

A WORLD OF EXTREMES

Can you imagine what it would be like to live and work among forty thousand poorest of the poor in a plot of land that measures about one square mile? Can you imagine *choosing* to do so, which would require leaving an affluent community and a successful career? This is the remarkable choice that Katie made when she left Hollywood for South Africa and founded Film School Africa, when her "normal" life began to shift.

Katie explained,

South Africa is a world of extremes: very different cultures pushing up against one another, very different socioeconomic backgrounds trying to work and live in close proximity. And because of the racially charged history, there is a real separation of cultures. This was very strange for me, since I grew up in Southern California which has the feel of a melting pot. So to be white and unafraid of crossing racial barriers was odd to many people, both black and white.

My job was very different too. I am now working with impoverished youth, and I was working with the Hollywood elite. That's a huge shift! My job went from having a sense of distance from those I worked with to being very intimate and involved with my students, literally wiping away tears and purposefully creating a space of vulnerability.

Food is different; the languages are different—we even drive on a different side of the road! It all takes getting used to, but when you're living the life you're called to live, eventually it all becomes . . . normal.

When Katie began living her dream, she encountered a number of ways in which she needed to grow and adapt. One growing edge she described was the typical way in which she was always looking for solutions to every problem she saw. She attributes that to being an American—a problem-solving culture. If something doesn't work, then you figure out why or discover what will.

Katie shared,

I needed to shift my thinking and understand that some issues require time and don't have easy solutions. The history and complexity of South Africa is vast and very different from the American experience, which has its own complex history. It's also been a challenge and growing experience learning when to help and when to allow my students to struggle, when to provide a platform that encourages growth and provides support, but where I don't swoop in and solve everything. I think that's been the biggest shift, but also the most rewarding.

When we hear about Katie and the adjustments she's made, it sounds like someone who has taken extreme risks and made huge sacrifices— and she has. Yet, if you met her, she would probably describe the process as more of "living" her way forward, one step at a time. Katie has leaned fiercely into her growing edge and expanded her capacity to live her dream in a place that has very little in common with the life she left behind.

YOUR GROWING EDGE

So, as you live into your dream it will be important for you to pay attention to the ways you're being stretched by your new normal—stretched toward your growing edge. Let me explain what I mean by "growing edge" through an experience I had one summer. I was meeting with one of my spiritual direction clients. As we sat together, considering her life situation, it was apparent that she was in a drought: personally, relationally, spiritually and vocationally life was dry and unyielding.

It didn't take long for me to associate the vivid images of a literal drought that surrounded me at the time in my own location. Indiana, like most Midwestern states, had experienced that particular summer a serious crisis of rainlessness. The leaves on the trees were wilted and drooping. Large limbs had fallen to the ground. Shrubs and grass were brown and crisp.

I "saw" as I listened to this woman's story the roots of a plant, forced by sheer necessity to penetrate the soil, hungrily bearing down in search of moisture in the ground water. I saw in this image a picture of this woman's "growing edge."

A growing edge is the place in our life where we are being pressed to deepen and develop. It might be from a drought of some kind or a new experience that requires something of us that we don't have to offer at present. It can come from experiencing too much or too little of something and having to adapt, narrow or expand. Whatever it is in life that applies the pressure, it usually doesn't feel comfortable. But rest assured it can cultivate an intense hunger and thirst and provide the fertile conditions that stimulate our roots to grow deeper into the soil of our true self in Christ.

REFLECTION: YOUR NEW NORMAL AND YOUR GROWING EDGE

Where is your growing edge right now? Where is this new dream you've launched exerting pressure to deepen and develop your capacity? Remember that it can often be in the very place that feels most dry or hard or overwhelming, a place you'd prefer to be transplanted from rather than remain. However, it just might be the enriched soil of your growing edge.

- Take some time to make a list of everything you identify as part of your "new normal." Review your list. What do you notice or learn from it?

- Now, consider using a mind map or clustering around the topic of your growing edge. Write down all the ways you are being stretched and deepened, expanded or contracted.

- After you capture your thoughts, zero in on one or two places that seem most significant. Think and reflect on how you can cooperate with God's invitation to grow in these areas. What will you do to learn and develop?

- If mind mapping is not a familiar term, figure 13.1 is an example. It happens to be my favorite planning tool.

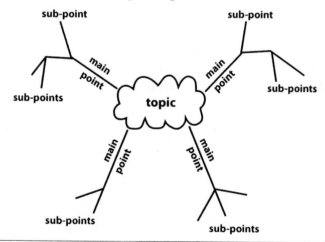

Fig. 13.1.

INTERVIEW

Sibyl Towner and the Springs

IVING BIRTH TO A DREAM CAN OFTEN feel like coming home. You feel as though you're being drawn toward a place within you that you've known about for a long time, a place that's been incubating, waiting for the right time to emerge. That's how it was for Dick and Sibyl Towner. Since early marriage, they'd dreamed about what it would be like to have a camp or retreat property for people to come to and be refreshed. Though Sibyl had worked for years in different camping ministries, the timing just never seemed right for both of them to embrace this vision. It wasn't until they began to feel a draw toward "home" that they realized it was also a draw toward this latent dream.

Dick and Sibyl had grown up in Cincinnati and lived there for half of their work life. Then they moved to Chicago and served on staff of Willow Creek Community Church. Dick developed and directed the Good $ense financial stewardship ministry for the next twenty years, and Sibyl served as a volunteer and on staff in a few different capacities—one of them in Willow's camping ministry. However, after a long and fruitful time there, Dick and Sibyl began to pine for "home."

Sibyl shared with me,

Dick began to feel restlessness inside him and said one day, "You know, I think we need to go back to Cincinnati. If we don't go soon, our return may be in a pine box" [a witty reference to the fact that their grave plots were there]. He knew his work was coming to an end at Willow. I felt the same thing. So, we took two years to close things out well—not knowing what we were preparing for.

"Not knowing what we were preparing for." Did you notice that phrase? It's interesting to observe that many who are called by God to move toward a dream often only know a general direction, a first step, but rarely more than that. Think about Abraham and Sarah: "Leave your native country, your relatives, and your father's family, and go to the land that I will show you" (Genesis 12:1). So, Dick and Sibyl began to make plans to return to Cincinnati. And they started to seek the counsel of good friends who knew them well.

We set the date to go back to Cincinnati and shared it with family and close friends, people who were for us and with us. And then they began to speak into our lives. One of them said, "If you come back, you should try to find and live in a place like 'Helen's cabin.'"

Helen was a friend of Sibyl and Dick's, and over the years had provided a tucked-away cabin where they would go "to be refreshed, do business with God and with each other." The idea appealed to them, and so they began to look for such a place, but had no clue where to start. They mentioned this to a friend, who in turn introduced them to Greg, a developer, who had a property and was looking for a partner to develop it with. So, Dick and Sibyl went with Greg to see the place, a 148-acre parcel of land with deep woods and a pond, as well as four existing cabins and a home. They fell in love with it, and soon after moved forward to purchase it with Greg. Everything seemed to be falling into place until the day they went to sign the final papers. Greg, for personal reasons, had to back out. Dick and Sibyl thought, *Now what?*

As they searched out God's purposes in this, they paused to consider another ministry they'd been involved with for some time, a ministry of help and healing for those who suffer from poverty and homelessness. They wondered if perhaps God was leading them in that direction, if that explained the abrupt closed door. Then one day, Sibyl asked Dick two profound questions: "How do you feel when you go down to the 'farm'?" as they called the property at the time. Dick responded, "I feel joy." "And how do you feel when you think about being called to the homeless ministry?" "I feel duty."

That was their answer. They both believed that the inner consolation and attraction to this place of retreat was the way of God for them. So, they brainstormed other people who might be interested in partnering with them to purchase the property that is now called "the Springs." A couple from Cincinnati came to mind whom they'd kept in contact with for the twenty years that they were away. Dick gave Linda Holmes a call and explained what was on his heart. Linda exclaimed, "Oh, my! Skip and I have dreamed about doing that!" A week later, on a Skype call to Bangkok, Thailand, where Skip was on business, the four of them had a conversation that led to a partnership to form a charitable foundation called "the Springs."

Since that time in 2010, Dick and Sibyl, along with the Skip and Linda Holmes, have hosted hundreds of folks who have made pilgrimage to this beautiful and remote property in Southeastern Indiana. They have moved toward joy, toward their love of creation and love in caring for this property and people. Though their geography is less populated, the Towners' still live lives populated with relationships, new friends and old, whom they welcome with grace and envelop with love. They have come home.

14

SUSTAINING

God gives us a vision and then He takes
us down to the valley to batter us into the shape
of the vision, and it is in the valley that so many of us faint and
give way. Whenever God gives you a vision, soak and soak and soak
continually in the one great truth of which you have had a vision; take it
to bed with you, sleep with it, rise up in the morning with it. Continually
bring your imagination into captivity to it and slowly and surely as the
months and years go by, God will make you one of His specialists in
that particular truth. By prayer and determination we have to
form the habit of keeping ourselves soaked in the vision
God has given us. Even if He has to batter us
into the shape of the vision.

Oswald Chambers

*I*F YOU'VE EVER PURCHASED A HOME, you may have experienced
the phenomenon that has been coined for such an occasion
called "buyer's regret." You sign what feels like a hundred and one papers
and simultaneously sign your life away. As much as you might have
fallen in the love with the property, or maybe just purchased it because

it was a good investment, or purchased it because you're practical and needed a place to live, there's something about making a thirty-year commitment that kind of takes your breath away.

Once you birth your dream and live into it for some time, you may also feel a twinge of "buyer's regret"—the sobering sense that you've taken something on, possibly for the next thirty years, that depends on your participation to sustain it. The choices you've made—the sacrifices and commitments and lifestyle changes—have all added up, and they have affected not just your work life or ministry life but all of your life. Because you are the instigator, what you have set in motion, with God's help and provision, feels like a big deal, and it begins to shape you—"batter you"—for better or for worse.

That's why it's important early on to begin to define some important rhythms that protect us from burning out or overextending, from allowing this dream to consume the whole plate of our lives to the point that there's no space left on the plate for anything else. Or the portions we give to other important relationships and needs have become much too small. It's certain that embracing a God-given dream will affect the whole of our lives: spiritual, relational, vocational, physical and recreational. And so, from time to time, we need to review and realign ourselves with the priorities that enable us to live a sustainable life as a dream builder. Developing intentional rhythms and a rule of life is one practice that will help us do that.

RHYTHMS AND A RULE OF LIFE

In recent years, more and more people outside monastic communities, where the concept of a rule of life originated, are talking about and working on a document that outlines the specific commitments they want to make to live a well-balanced, nourished and fruitful life. These commitments are daily, weekly, monthly and yearly rhythms related to our spiritual, relational, vocational, physical and recreational well-being. They describe the kind of lifestyle we want to live—in humble dependence on God, in full admission of our humanity—necessary commitments in order to live fully and wholeheartedly. Author and poet David Whyte is often quoted as saying, "The antidote for exhaustion is not rest; it's wholeheartedness." A rule of life helps us create the conditions that keep our hearts whole.

The term *rule of life* originates from the Benedictine tradition and a book written by their founder, Benedict of Nursia (A.D. 480–547). The book is an extensive description of how a monastic community should function and how individuals within that community should conduct themselves. Today, some of the key aspects of the Benedictine Rule have been extracted and adapted by writers like Steve Macchia and Mark Buchanan, in *Crafting a Rule of Life: An Invitation to a Well-Ordered Way,* and Ruth Haley Barton, in *Sacred Rhythms: Arranging Our Lives for Spiritual Transformation.*

A rule of life helps us recognize that our lives really aren't composed of compartments with labels on each drawer, but rather the parts of our lives have contiguous relationships, each one affecting, pressing into and influencing the others parts. Like a honeycomb, all the segments of life are interconnected, and the sap of our life flows between and through each to the others.

The dream that you initiated can influence how much sleep you get. It can provide or consume financial resources. It will require hard work and can take time away from key relationships as well as require you to forge new ones. Your dream can occupy the space you had to ride bikes, do woodworking or read a novel. It can fuel your spiritual life and how you pray or whether you pray. You will experience God through living your dream or sometimes feel as though God has become distant as you toil over your dream. Because you've said yes to such an ambitious and life-altering decision as a dream, it's prudent for you to sit down, as soon as you have a moment, and wrestle with how your dream is affecting your life and what rhythms you want to put in place in order for your life and dream to be sustained.

SPRINGS OF LIVING WATER

When Sibyl and Dick Towner relocated to a remote property in Southeastern Indiana to direct the Springs, many of their friends wondered how they'd do. Those who knew them wondered how Sibyl and Dick would survive somewhat isolated from people, after living in Cincinnati and Chicago, and living active, extraverted lives in those cities. One of the first things Dick and Sibyl determined was to commit to a rule of life that would help sustain them.

As odd as it might sound, one of the first commitments of their rule of life involved choosing to not only work at the Springs but retreat there as well. Retreat for them had always been a practice of repairing, bringing the life they'd been living and the life God longed for them to live in review. Remember Helen's Cabin, where they would go away to do business with God and one another? So the Towners very consciously made a commitment to take regular time to retreat at the Springs for their own soulish and spiritual well-being.

In addition, they have also developed some important rhythms related to daily life. These have been in the making over their lifetime and have become especially important today as they create a haven of rest for others. Sibyl described some of their daily rhythms to me:

> One of the ways of sustaining our lives is by having a slow start in the morning. We use the mornings for exercise (we walk most days), an unhurried breakfast, lingering with God and in the Word, and then we let the day unfold. We pray the divine hours [a monastic term describing set times of prayer], we do compline at night, and we always go to bed together. Dick also has a discipline of writing down three things he's thankful for each day. Prayerfully ending and beginning each day is part of our rhythm.

I've known Sibyl for a couple of years now and have been drawn to her, to the deep reservoir of love, spiritual vitality and wisdom that flows from her. I know her as a person who pours out her life for Jesus and the sake of others. I wasn't surprised by her responses when I asked her to describe her own rule of life. Most of the time, however, she used the pronoun *we*—a testament to the solidarity of their fifty-plus year marriage.

Dick and Sibyl have a vision and desire that the Springs be a setting where they can "welcome the weary to a time and place of rest in the beautiful surroundings of nature and in the presence of our ever-present

God." They have welcomed many weary souls—strangers and friends—who somehow found their way to this off-the-beaten-path haven. To offer others rest, Dick and Sibyl know that they have to live from a place of rest within themselves. And so they practice a rule of life in order to sustain a deep center, full of rest and joy, with their only plan of retiring involving a pine box.

BECOMING STEWARDS OF OUR LIVES

One of our great concerns when we began Sustainable Faith Indy was what it would be like to have people around—a lot. We cherish and need alone time, and time as a couple and with our family. We know that we need solitude with God and with ourselves, time to stare out the window or sit on our front porch uninterrupted and to be still. So, right away, we began to wrestle with our capacity and what would allow us the space we need to give from full hearts, rather than ragged hearts worn thin.

Our resolve has been tested and I will come clean and say that I'm the more vulnerable one to compromise what we have agreed is best for us and our families. I am a pleaser and helper, and have a difficult time saying no to people who ask things of me. More than once, I have brought this issue to my spiritual director, sharing with Nancy the struggle I have with drawing boundaries and saying no, and respecting my own spiritual, relational and physical capacity.

Many of us will hesitate or renege on the responsibility to manage the most important resource that will sustain our dream: ourselves! We neglect guarding the output of our lives by ensuring sufficient input. There's a notion we have in our fast-paced, frenetic culture that we are victims of busyness. Somehow we believe that we have no control over the pace and extent of our energy expenditures. The truth is, we are not victims but co-conspirators! We choose, daily, to overextend, run ourselves ragged and ring ourselves out from too much going, doing, working, fretting, talking, buying and reaching. It's time we put a stake in the ground and become stewards of our own lives.

To steward our lives means that we take responsibility to invest ourselves wisely and wholeheartedly toward the life and work that God has called us to. To be a steward, we must pay attention to how much we give (output) and how much we receive (input) through our work, relationships and play. *Balance* is a common word we choose to describe the ratios we strive to achieve. While there is something satisfying about the word and the idea of balance, it can also be misleading. The parts of our lives can't be measured equally. Some weigh more than others. At different times in life, some have more priority than at other times. For instance, if you are a parent of young children, those relationships place more weight on you now then they will when your kids are grown. So, to create balance really means to make sure that the output of our lives is balanced by sufficient input.

A way to think about this is to ask yourself, What do I need more of? And what do I need less of?

You can ask these questions of any aspect of your life—physical, spiritual, relational and so forth. When you ask, What do I need more of physically? you might answer, sleep. What do I need less of physically? you might answer, sitting at my desk working on my computer. This less of/more of principle can help you identify your needs and create rhythms of life that establish better balance between your output and input.

For instance, if we apply the input-output principle to the previous example of our physical needs, we might decide to commit to go to bed at 10 on weeknights. We might also establish a habit of setting a timer that reminds us to get up from our desk and take a ten minute walk or standing break every two hours. By this, we are helping create balance between how much we give physically and how we replenish physically what we've given.

In regard to replenishing, one thing I've observed is that when I become exhausted and depleted, it often feels like it will take a month to recover. In reality, I've found that having a couple slow mornings or an afternoon bike ride or a walk in a nature preserve does wonders to refill and refuel my heart, mind, body and soul. It doesn't always take as much time as we think to recover what we've spent. Learning to take small, daily drinks can sustain the equilibrium of the whole of our lives.

So, I'd like to recommend that as a final exercise of this book you think through the different aspects of your life and how you might design daily, weekly, monthly and yearly rhythms that help you maintain balance between your input and output. This is a modified version of a rule of life and a good start toward helping you establish margin and balance. As you work through it, keep in mind that it's better to not be overly ambitious and become defeated from the onset. Start simple.

Once you have worked through the process, it would be valuable to share it with several in your immediate circle—family, friends, a spiritual director or mentor—and ask them to help you live in accordance with your rule.

REFLECTION: MY RHYTHMS AND RULE OF LIFE

Table 14.1. Rhythms and Rule of Life

	Daily Rhythms	Weekly Rhythms	Monthly Rhythms	Yearly Rhythms
Spiritual What do I need more of?				
Spiritual What do I need less of?				
Physical What do I need more of?				
Physical What do I need less of?				
Relational What do I need more of?				
Relational What do I need less of?				
Vocational What do I need more of?				
Vocational What do I need less of?				
Recreational What do I need more of?				
Recreational What do I need less of?				

Epilogue

WHAT COMES OF DREAMS

I'm working on a building
I'm working on a building
I'm working on a building
For my Lord, for my Lord.

African American Spiritual

SUSPECT THAT MOST OF THE TIME, those who have been given a task from God to realize a dream have only a hint of why and what it all means—all it adds up to. Take for instance a man I've never met but heard was a pastor, who bought our house ten years ago on a short-sale. What was he thinking when he came into this abandoned home and saw with his own eyes both the potential and the disrepair of a home left to rot? Did he know that one day a couple would come along and call the work he did "sacred"? Did he have any notion that he was "working on a building for his Lord"—like the words to the song in the epigraph suggest? When he spent time examining the bones of this old house, was he conscious or unconscious that he was preparing a manger of sorts, a place where people would come to draw closer to Jesus?

My guess is that he might have had a premonition of good things to come. However, I doubt that he was aware, as he went to work utilizing his gifts with a standard of excellence we are so grateful for today that he was working on a building for our Lord. He was. And as we have inhabited our space and received the countless gifts of its goodness, we are amazed at how perfectly it fits the needs of Sustainable Faith Indy.

For instance, the entry way is flanked by two extra-large doorways opening into the great room on the right and the dining room on the left and provides a wide and gracious welcome as guests enter. The butler's pantry is now open into the dining room, a pass way and perfect spot for a drink station, including the commercial coffee maker we have installed. Both sides provide a galley for our guests to come and refill drinks and grab snacks as they retreat. The den off the great room still has the original beveled glass French doors and provides beautiful space for me and David to offer spiritual direction. It is both private and quiet—but suitable and comfortable for our male and female directees. The two HVAC systems installed during the renovation were a gift as we finished out the third floor and added two guest rooms and a bath. The master bedroom suite was also a bonus as it provides a private sitting area for us when we need a place to get away. Not only are there many features of this home that make it ideal for our purposes, the ambiance is unique; the gracious, solid, sacred feel is exactly what we had envisioned and for which we had prayed.

In a significant way, the man who renovated this home was cooperating with God in an unknowing way. And so you and I might be doing the same. We have put our hand to the plow, we are working on the building, and we have no idea what may come of our work. We don't know in what way we are collaborating with another or bigger or smaller purpose than the one we can see.

This is sacred work. The creative work of starting something new—of bringing God's vision to life—is a holy calling and one that can prepare the way for other dreamers. As you embark on your journey of giving birth to your dream, work hard, do excellent work, and take time to notice those foreshadowing moments when you have the niggling suspicion that you are uncovering a gift that God has for you to find and nurturing it for a far more significant and generative purpose than you even realize today.

As you do, I'd like to conclude by offering this prayer of blessing over you and me and our work:

We have witnessed inspiration of spirit
in the voice of a woman,
in the colours of an artist,
in the prophetic vision of a leader,
in the most simple acts of daily kindness.
We have experienced creativity in our own soul,
in seeing things anew,
in unplanned utterances of wonder and passion,
in the most ordinary actions of tending and caring.
In the life of the world this night,
in every nation and among every people,
let there be fresh stirrings of your Spirit.
In our own soul and in the soul of the world tonight
let there be fresh stirrings of your mighty creating Spirit.
Amen

ACKNOWLEDGMENTS

*Y*OU MIGHT WONDER WHY AUTHORS are typically compelled to include in their books a long list of people to acknowledge. I suppose it's because when you finish such a monumental task as writing a book, and you stop and sigh and take a big breath, you are aware of how you couldn't do what you do without the support of many, many people.

I first and foremost want to thank my nearest and dearest family: David, my sweet companion and shareholder of this dream; my daughters Britt, Bri and Brooke Ellen; my son, Brandt, and his wife, Laura, my grandest gifts on earth—Eli, Riley and Harper Lillian; and my parents-in-law, Dave and Marlene. The longer I live, the more aware I am of this most blessed gift—my family.

I also want to thank and acknowledge people who through their close friendship, encouragement and beautiful lives contribute so richly to mine. These are the folks who have listened to our hearts, prayed and cried with and for us, and supported us along the way of realizing our dream. Some have hosted showers for Sustainable Faith Indy, and some have even put together IKEA furniture for our guest rooms! Many, many thanks to Tim and Mary Byers, Nate and Megan Hershey, Steve and Samantha Spencer, Ann Reynolds, Brent Croxton, Dave and Jody Nixon, Todd Fisher (our pastor), Jim Matthias and Jen Friesen, Randy Reese, Rob Loane and Pam Edwards (my VP3 pals).

In addition, I want to thank publically, from the bottom of my heart, my dear friend Pam Sechrist, who went way beyond the call of duty as our realtor; and Anne Grizzle, whose meaningful texts through our birthing process always seemed to come at the right time. I am also grateful for my friends Sandra Herron and Steve Ingram, who shared their organizational brilliance and strategic planning expertise with me. And sincere thanks to Joe and Lisa Miller for their valued friendship and for Joe's legal counsel.

A group that has graced our retreat space almost every Monday night for the first two years of its being has become very dear to me. Many thanks and much gratitude for my Journey group: Pam, Jody, Christin, Liz, Denise, Missie, Martina, Kim, Michele, Lisa, Stacey and Savannah.

As a spiritual director I am also grateful for the one who holds my story with me and offers compassionate, wise support: my spiritual director, Nancy Campbell.

And to all of my directees—you know your names—but out of regard for your privacy, I won't include them. You've given me so much by entrusting me with your spiritual journeys.

I'd also like to sincerely thank all of those I had the privilege to interview. I regret that I was not able to include everyone's dream in my book. Just the same, I am more convinced than ever through your sharing your dreams with me that God is up to something very good in our world. Thank you to Abby Kuzma, Chris Smith, Dave Baldwin, Joanna Taft, Katie Taylor, Kelly Hartman, Liz Alig, MaryBeth Jackson, Mary Freeman, Nate Hershey, Phileena Heuertz, Rachael Lagarde, Sibyl Towner, Randy Reese, Melissa Millis, Suzy Roth and Tom Durant.

A special thanks to Rob and Deb Wingerter, and Ron and Allison Wingerter—owners and innkeepers of Mahseh Center—a beautiful and tranquil place of retreat, and where much of this book was written.

And finally, I'd like to express my gratitude to InterVarsity Press and all the staff involved in publishing this book. It's hard to imagine being more at home with any other publisher.

Thank you, especially, to Cindy Bunch for her belief in me, my message and my writing. If it weren't for Cindy inviting me to a writing retreat and letting me bring my husband along, our dream might never have come to be! Sincere thanks, as well, to Jeff Crosby and his team for the amazing support and excellence for which they do their marketing work.

Most gratefully, Beth

Appendix

WEB RESOURCES

The following are web addresses for each of the individuals I interviewed:

City Life Wheels, www.ciyfc.org/ministries/city_life_wheels (Nate Hershey)
Eco Café Haiti, www.ecocafehaiti.com (Tom Durant)
Englewood Review of Books, www.englewoodreview.org (Chris Smith)
Film School Africa, http://filmschoolafrica.org (Katie Taylor)
Furnace Hills Coffee, www.furnacehillscoffee.com (Dave Baldwin)
Gravity Center, http://gravitycenter.com (Phileena Heuertz)
Hands of Hope Orphan and Adoption Care, www.gracehandsofhope.org
    (Suzy Roth)
Harrison Center for the Arts, http://harrisoncenter.org (Joanna Taft)
Liz Alig Fashion, www.lizalig.com (Elizabeth Roney)
Neighborhood Christian Legal Clinic, www.nclegalclinic.org or Abigail
    .Kuzma@atg.in.gov (Abby Kuzma)
Nou Hope Haiti, www.nouhopehaiti.org or info.nouhopehaiti@gmail.com
    (Melissa Millis)
The Springs, www.thespringsindiana.org (Sibyl Towner)
VantagePoint3, http://vantagepoint3.org (Randy Reese)
The Viewfinder Project, www.theviewfinderproject.com (MaryBeth Jackson)

NOTES

INTRODUCTION

p. 18   "the clarity paradox": Gregory McKeown, "The Disciplined Pursuit of Less," *Harvard Business Review Blog Network*, blogs.hbr .org/2012/08/the-disciplined-pursuit-of-less.

p. 20   "way leads to way": Robert Frost, "The Road Not Taken," 1916.

CHAPTER 2: BROODING

p. 44   "a deeply held belief that possesses the worth to influence": Randy Reese and Rob Loane, *The Journey* (Sioux Falls, SD: VantagePoint3, 2009), p. 92.

CHAPTER 3: WELCOMING

p. 47   "Months prior to setting out on the Camino": Phileena Heuertz, *Pilgrimage of a Soul: Contemplative Spirituality for the Active Life* (Downers Grove, IL: InterVarsity Press, 2010), p. 29.

CHAPTER 4: DISCERNING

p. 60   "What is giving me a touchstone": Lois A. Lindbloom, *Companions on the Journey: Cultivating Discernment in Spiritual Direction* (Northfield, MN: Lois A. Lindbloom, 2010), p. 15.

p. 63   "Many of us face a dilemma when trying to deal with a personal problem, question, or decision." Parker Palmer, "The Clearness Committee," Center for Courage and Renewal, www.courage renewal.org/parker/writings/clearness-committee.

CHAPTER 5: NAMING

p. 69   "The true voyage of discovery": Marcel Proust, *In Search of Lost Time*, vol. 5 (Boston: Centaur Editions, 2013).

CHAPTER 6: SHAPING

p. 81   "The work which I do does not make me": Martin Luther, quoted
             by James Houston, *The Mentored Life: From Individualism to Per-
             sonhood* (Carol Stream, IL: NavPress, 2002), p. 115.

CHAPTER 7: SORTING

p. 90   "There are all different kinds of voices calling you": Frederick
             Buechner, *Listening to Your Life: Daily Meditations with Frederick
             Buechner* (New York: HarperCollins, 1992), p. 185.

CHAPTER 8: CHANGING

p. 99   "the notion that it is wrong for one to change his mind": Michael,
             "The Virtue of Flip-Flopping," This I Believe, November 5, 2011,
             http://thisibelieve.org/essay/107609. Michael is a high school
             student from Wolcott, Connecticut.

CHAPTER 9: WAITING

p. 111   "Sooner or later, if you are on any classic 'spiritual schedule'":
             Richard Rohr, *Falling Upward: Spirituality for the Two Halves of Life*
             (Hoboken, NJ: Jossey-Bass, 2011), pp. 65-66.
p. 115   "The action of God on our lives": Margaret Silf, *Inner Compass: An
             Invitation to Ignatian Spirituality* (Chicago: Loyola Press, 1999), p.
             86.

CHAPTER 10: DYING

p. 120   "led to the edge of your own private resources": Richard Rohr,
             Falling Upward: Spirituality for the Two Halves of Life (Hoboken,
             NJ: Jossey-Bass, 2011), pp. 65.
p. 124   "Life-Fate-God-Grace-Mystery": Ibid.
p. 125   "The seed must rest in the earth": Caryll Houselander, *Little Way of
             the Infant Jesus* (Manchester, NH: Sophia Institute Press, 2012).

CHAPTER 11: RESURRECTING

p. 133   "new life comes slowly, awkwardly, on wobbly wings": Sue Monk
             Kidd, *When the Soul Waits: Spiritual Direction for Life's Sacred Ques-
             tions* (Grand Rapids: HarperCollins, 2007), p. 177.

CHAPTER 12: BIRTHING

p. 147   "The action of God on our lives": Margaret Silf, *Inner Compass: An Invitation to Ignatian Spirituality* (Chicago: Loyola Press, 1999), p. 86.

CHAPTER 13: LIVING

p. 155   "We do not think ourselves into a new way of living": Richard Rohr, the eighth core principle of the Center for Action and Contemplation.

CHAPTER 14: SUSTAINING

p. 163   "The antidote to exhaustion isn't rest; it's wholeheartedness": David Whyte, *Crossing the Unknown Sea: Work as a Pilgrimage of Identity* (New York: Riverhead Trade, 2002), p. 132.

EPILOGUE

p. 171   "We have witnessed inspiration of spirit": John Philip Newell, "Thursday Night Prayer: Prayers of Thanksgiving and Intercession" in *Sounds of the Eternal: A Celtic Psalter* (San Antonio, TX: New Beginnings, 2012), p. 58.

ALSO BY BETH A. BOORAM

Awaken Your Senses
978-0-8308-3560-7

formatio

TRADITION. EXPERIENCE.
TRANSFORMATION.

Formatio books from InterVarsity Press follow the rich tradition of the church in the journey of spiritual formation. These books are not merely about being informed, but about being transformed by Christ and conformed to his image. Formatio stands in InterVarsity Press's evangelical publishing tradition by integrating God's Word with spiritual practice and by prompting readers to move from inward change to outward witness. InterVarsity Press uses the chambered nautilus for Formatio, a symbol of spiritual formation because of its continual spiral journey outward as it moves from its center. We believe that each of us is made with a deep desire to be in God's presence. Formatio books help us to fulfill our deepest desires and to become our true selves in light of God's grace.